D1526817

A CENTURY OF SERVICE

Booker T. Washington Monument, Tuskegee University, Tuskegee, Alabama.
Courtesy of Office Sponsored Programs and Media Center, Tuskegee
University, Tuskegee, Alabama.

A CENTURY OF SERVICE

LAND-GRANT COLLEGES AND UNIVERSITIES, 1890-1990

Edited by

Ralph D. Christy
Lionel Williamson

Transaction Publishers
New Brunswick (U.S.A.) and London (U.K.)

Copyright © 1992 by Transaction Publishers. New Brunswick, New Jersey 08903

All rights reserved under International and Pan-American Copyright Conventions. No part of this book may be reproduced or transmitted in any form or by any means, electronic or mechanical, including photocopy, recording, or any information storage and retrieval system, without prior permission in writing from the publisher. All inquiries should be addressed to Transaction Publishers, Rutgers—The State University, New Brunswick, New Jersey 08903

Library of Congress Catalog Number: 91-14588
ISBN: 1-56000-002-3
Printed in the United States of America

Library of Congress Cataloging-in-Publication Data

A Century of Service: Land-Grant Colleges and Universities 1890–1990 / edited by Ralph D. Christy and Lionel Williamson.

    p. cm.

"The collection of readings in this work emanated from papers presented at the 1989 annual meeting of the American Agricultural Economics Association held at Southern University and A&M College in Baton Rouge, Louisiana"—Pref.

Includes bibliographical references and index.
ISBN 1-56000-002-3

1. Universities and colleges, Black—United States—History—Congresses. 2. State universities and colleges—United States—History—Congresses. I. Christy, Ralph D. II. Williamson, Lionel, 1943– . III. American Agricultural Economics Association. LC2781.C46 1991
378'.054'0973—dc20

91-14588
CIP

Contents

Preface

When Congress passed the First Morrill Act in 1862, a new chapter in the history of higher education began. This legislation marked the birth of a publicly supported higher education system in the United Stated that provided for much wider participation by American citizens.

The intent of this Act was to provide to all citizens of America access to institutions of higher learning. Yet, in spite of this noble effort, the southern states continued to ignore the academic needs of its African American population. Even though Alcorn University was reestablished in 1878 as a Land-Grant institution under the First Morrill Act, it suffered from the lack of financial support necessary for it to flourish. However, its reaffirmation under the Second Morrill Act of 1890 marked the beginning of an almost unbelievable century of accomplishments in the annals of higher education.

The passage of the Second Morrill Act of 1890 provided the impetus for southern states to open and support public higher education institutions for "people of color." Now, for one hundred years, these Historically Black Colleges and Universities (HBCUs) have assumed and continued to maintain a unique and important role in providing educational opportunities for thousands of students to whom no other doors would have been opened. They have made better the odds that all Americans would have access to a higher education.

The 1890 Land-Grant institutions are a legacy of what can be accomplished with little more than a determined, tenacious commitment to survive and excel. Thus, to be a part of any project that commemorates the survival of the 1890 Land-Grant Colleges and Universities, is a privilege and an overwhelming honor. This book, *A Century of Service: The 1890 Land-Grant Colleges and Universities*, is a fitting and welcomed celebration of a one hundred year old miracle.

Created in the shadows of slavery for the purpose of separating American citizens along racial lines in the higher education arena, the 1890 Land-Grant Colleges and Universities were given their early historic mission by the United States Supreme Court's decision in *Plessy v. Ferguson*. Although "separate-but-equal" was the court's edict, its effect and application permitted separate educational opportunities and a great deal of inequality. The establishment and subsequent funding of the 1890 institutions affirmed under the Second Morrill Act offered a blueprint for their certain failure. The channeling of their funds through the states' treasuries, along with those appropriated for the 1862 institutions, created a funding system that was inadequate for the support and development of quality academic programs, for the payment of reasonable salaries to teaching and support personnel, and for the building of necessary research, academic, and administrative facilities. This served to hinder, but not to stop, the growth of these HBCUs.

In spite of the inequality in the financing of academic and support programs in the 1890 Land-Grant institutions, they have succeeded in establishing and building quality resident academic and extension programs in the areas of agriculture, home economics, the mechanical arts, and other professional fields that are on par with those of other colleges and universities not suffering the same economic, social, man-power, and facility limitations. As noted throughout this work, with meager resources, the 1890 institutions have amassed an impressive record of achievement in the areas of agriculture research, cooperative extension, development of rural communities support systems, human resources development, resident instruction, international development, and technology and information transfer.

The collection of readings in this work emanated from papers presented at the 1989 annual meeting of the American Agricultural Economics Association held at Southern University and A & M College in Baton Rouge, Louisiana. They chronicle the contributions of the 1890 HBCUs to the betterment of the lot of mankind. Regardless of whether one views this as a historical sojourn or a contemporary prospectus, the message is the same—these institutions have endured because of a commitment to service and excellence in academic and research programs.

The contributors are a conglomerate of academicians, researchers, extension personnel, agriculture specialists, higher education administrators and, for the most part, products of land-grant institutions. Thus, those who are fortunate to read this eclectic publication are certain to discern it as a labor of love, loyalty, and dedication aimed at projecting the spirit that has characterized the 1890 Land-Grant Colleges and Universities.

The editors, Ralph D. Christy and Lionel Williamson, are to be congratulated for their foresight in recognizing the value of maintaining these documents for posterity's sake. Theirs is an obvious effort to insure complete and comprehensive coverage of the facets of the 1890 Land-Grant institutions that have made such institutions great, even as the odds were against their ever reaching that level.

Those of us who support the continued longevity and success of the 1890 schools are indeed grateful for this work and owe much to those who have given their time and talent to assure the successful compilation of *A Century of Service: The 1890 Land-Grant Colleges and Universities.*

DOLORES R. SPIKES
President, Southern University System
and Chancellor, SUBR

Acknowledgments

Publication of these conference proceedings resulted from the efforts of a large number of individuals and organizations. A project of this sort cannot escape such a debt. At the American Agricultural Economics Association (AAEA) meetings in Reno in 1986, the Committee on the Opportunities and Status of Blacks in Agricultural Economics (COS-BAE) formed a subgroup whose task was to plan the Association's involvement in the 1890 Land-Grant Colleges and Universities Century of Service Celebrations. This subgroup consisted of Lionel Williamson (co-chair), Ralph D. Christy (co-chair), Joyce Allen, T. T. Williams, Sidney Evans, and Leroy Davis. Through the able leadership of Joyce Allen (past chairperson, COSBAE), the subgroup's tasks were further defined (1) to coordinate our preconference activities with those of other organizations (U.S. Department of Agriculture [USDA], Association of Black Land-Grant Administrators, and other professional agricultural associations), and (2) to expand the committee's involvement in the centennial celebrations by recognizing contributions of black agricultural economists.

In February 1988, the preconference proposal was presented in the New Orleans meetings of COSBAE, and by August of that year, in Knoxville, a preconference program was approved by the committee. The AAEA Board endorsed this program at its fall meetings in 1988. A portion of the committee's professional involvement recognized "Outstanding Black Agricultural Economists," and Sidney Evans and Al Parks gave consideration to the definition of "Early Black Agricultural Economists." Doris Newton provided leadership, establishing criteria for selecting and developing a brochure listing "The Outstanding Black Agricultural Economists," which was published in the spring of 1990.

These two activities, the preconference and brochure, were made possible by the generous support of several organizations: the Ford Foundation, Farm Foundation, AAEA Foundation, and Economic Research Service, USDA.

The Department of Agricultural Economics at Southern University deserves our appreciation for its efforts in hosting the conference. Pat McLean-Meyinsse and Leroy Davis served as local committee chairpersons who helped gain support for such a conference on their campus. Many other individuals at Southern played a major role in hosting this conference: Adell Brown, Abdulhakeem Y. Salaam, Tammy Golden-Armand, Tesfa G. Gebremedhin, Dewitt Jones (chair, Department of Agricultural Economics), and Bobby Phills (dean, College of Agriculture). President Dolores Spikes of Southern University was most gracious in extending to us the University's facilities, including her home, and providing the conference's opening remarks.

We received special support beyond the call of duty from Lester Manderscheid and Sandra Batie (AAEA past presidents); Carlton Davis and Paul Farris (AAEA Foundation board members); and Joyce Allen and Handy Williamson, Jr. (past and current COSBAE chairpersons, respectively). These individuals served as a ground swell of valuable information and pillars of support as they provided constructive, useful, and thoughtful feedback during critical junctures of this project.

Finally, special recognition is given to Sharon Wyllie and Susan Duhe for their clerical support, Patricia Santos for assistance with the preconference program, and Elin Epperson for editorial expertise given to completing these proceedings.

Introduction
A Century Of Service: The Past, Present, and Future Roles of 1890 Land-Grant Colleges and Institutions

Ralph D. Christy, Lionel Williamson, and Handy Williamson, Jr.

This year the 1890 Land-Grant Institutions will celebrate a century of service to their clientele and to the nation. With the passage of enabling legislation (second Morrill Act, 1890), these colleges and universities were established to provide training to African Americans in the fields of agriculture, home economics, the mechanical arts, and other useful professions. Under the premise of legal separation of the races in the South, they were established in response to the earlier development of the Land-Grant System in 1862 (first Morrill Act). Today, sixteen 1890 Land-Grant Institutions and Tuskegee University remain actively engaged in carrying out their Land-Grant mission.

The Committee on the Opportunities and Status of Blacks in Agricultural Economics (COSBAE) of the American Agricultural Economics Association (AAEA) was pleased to initiate the preconference program from which these proceedings emerged. The goal of the conference was to recognize the contributions of 1890 Land-Grant Institutions and to highlight the Agricultural Economics and Rural Development programs at these colleges and universities. Specifically, the conference had four objectives: (1) to provide an overview of the historical development of the 1890 Institutions; (2) to present a current description of the resident instruction, research, extension, and international development programs at these schools; (3) to offer views of future roles which 1890 institutions will play; and (4) to suggest alternative institutional designs for 1890 institutions, in particular their colleges of agriculture, in order to enhance the status and opportunities for African American agricultural scientists and professionals.

As the 1890 Land-Grant colleges and universities celebrate a century of service, many new challenges in this post-civil-rights era emerge. These challenges are multidimensional, having significant implications for the changing economic, social, and political realities for African Americans and for the nation at large. In keeping with the Land-Grant mission, development of human capital through formal education, development of knowledge, and dissemination of information are necessary for the full participation of African Americans. While building upon their strengths and traditions, 1890 institutions are not only seeking to maintain an identity in an environment that is dynamic and complex, but also to develop capabilities in areas where other institutions have committed little or no resources.

Because of the unique economic characteristics of education and a philosophy which advocates accessible educational opportunities for the masses, government has played a significant role in the development of institutions for higher learning in the United States. Historically, state and local governments have provided greater support for schools than the federal government has. Notable exceptions are the federal involvement given to Land-Grant Institutions, the civil rights obligations required by the Supreme Court (*Brown v. Board of Education*, 1954), the aerospace initiatives taken as a result of the launching of Sputnik in 1957, and the war on poverty established by the Economic Opportunity Act in 1964 (Jaynes and Williams, 1989). Although state governments initially were reluctant to provide full support for 1890 Land-Grant Institutions, in more recent years they have placed greater emphasis on education, motivated by a strategy to enhance economic development and to facilitate efficiency and coordination in allocating and using public funds for higher education. The federal government, on the other hand, has pursued a strategy enhancing and developing Historically Black Colleges and Universities (HBCUs) to ensure educational opportunities for all citizens. The future of the 1890 institutions and of educational opportunities available to African Americans will no doubt be determined by the actions of government at both levels, national and state.

A comprehensive study documenting the educational goals, strategies, and programs of African Americans reached the following conclusions relevant to excellence and equal educational opportunities (ibid.):

1. Substantial progress has been made toward the provision of high-quality, equal, and integrated education.
2. Compensatory education programs—Head Start and Chapter I—have overall positive (although sometimes short-term) effects on the academic achievement of disadvantaged students.
3. Persistent and large gaps in the schooling, quality, and achievement outcomes of education for blacks and whites exist.
4. Schools do substantially affect the amount of learning that takes place.
5. Blacks' status in higher education, as undergraduates, graduates, and faculty, has worsened or stalled since the mid-1970s.
6. Separation and differential treatment of blacks continue to be widespread in the elementary and secondary schools and in different forms in institutions of higher learning.

Conclusions five and six have particular implications for 1890 institutions. The number of undergraduate degrees earned by African Americans has declined continuously since 1976, representing the greatest losses of all ethnic groups (Carter and Wilson, 1989). Among African American students, male students' college completion rates have declined much faster than African American female students. This downward trend also appeared in post graduate studies: a 31.8 percent loss in masters degrees and a 22.1 percent loss in doctoral degrees from 1978 to 1988 (ibid.). HBCUs awarded 35.8 percent of the African American bachelors degrees in 1987. The number of degrees awarded by HBCUs declined by 8.2 percent between 1982 and 1987, largely due to the closing, the merging, or the changing status of schools (ibid.). Significant losses in African American college graduation rates, particularly at the graduate school level, suggest further declines in African American representation on faculties within the nation's colleges and universities. With the absence of positive role models at many colleges and universities, African American students often experience social alienation and racial discrimination (Steele, 1989). Therefore, an important challenge to 1890 institutions (and to all institutions of higher learning) is to increase the enrollment, retention, and graduation rates of African American students.

Beyond the above-mentioned challenges within our universities and colleges, the mission of 1890 institutions has also been to create and disseminate information to farmers and rural residents in order to enhance their quality of life. This mission has been accomplished through the institutions' research and extension programs which have developed a reputation for a unique expertise in providing technical assistance to all limited resource rural clientele, both farm and nonfarm. In serving the needs of the African American farmers, however, 1890 institutions must also recognize the tremendous structural change brought about by technological and institutional forces. African American farmers have been leaving production agriculture over the past three decades at a rate twice that of white farmers. Many of the remaining farmers, on average, have limited resources and are relatively smaller, in terms of land and sales volumes, than white farmers.

Serving the needs of nonfarm rural Americans has likewise been subject to socioeconomic and technical transformations, which have influenced the research and outreach programs at 1890 institutions. Demographic realities have been such that while a significant number of African Americans have relocated to urban areas, 90 percent of all rural African American residents live in the South (Litcher and Heaton, 1986). Since the late 1970s one of the important characteristics of this rural population is the rising poverty rates (Sawhill, 1988; Moen, 1989). In 1987, 44 percent of all African Americans living in rural areas were below the poverty line (U.S. Department of Commerce, 1989). Moreover, many counties in the rural South have experienced persistent poverty as defined by the United States Department of Agriculture (USDA; Bellamy and Ghelfi, 1989). This important trend in rural America suggests further challenges for the 1890 colleges and universities.

Given these important trends in higher education, agriculture, and nonfarm rural society, it is imperative that we understand and clarify the important contributions of 1890 institutions to a nation which is undergoing radical transformations. To do so, then, the following presentations have been organized around the four objectives of the conference:

to present (1) the historical background, (2) current issues, (3) future directions, and (4) alternative institutional designs of the 1890 institutions.

Historical Background

Although the HBCUs were authorized under the first Morrill Act of 1862, only Mississippi and Kentucky established institutions under this act, and only Alcorn State University, in Mississippi, was designated as "Land-Grant." In 1890 a second Morrill Act was passed specifically to support black Land-Grant Institutions (see table I.1). As a result, those Southern states which did not have such an institution established one. Tennessee State University, established in 1909, was the last of these.

Currently, seventeen institutions, located predominantly in the southeast region of the United States, are considered as the "1890 Land-Grant Institutions" (see figure I.1). Of these seventeen, Tuskegee University is a private university, although it is normally considered one of the HBCUs because, along with most of the others, it was created by an act of state or territorial legislation (see table I.2 for historical data).

Although most of the black Land-Grant Institutions were established following the Civil War and before 1900, their growth and development was restricted by lack of financial resources. This lack of support for research and only modest support for teaching continued until after World War II. At that time both public and private funding agencies became more sensitive to the needs of these institutions. Included in this new awareness was the need to provide support for the research aspirations of faculty at these schools. As a result, over the twenty-five year period from 1942 to 1967, several initiatives not only encouraged but actually facilitated research at the 1890 institutions. From 1947 to 1952, for example, Fort Valley State University in Georgia participated in joint research activities with Atlanta University with research funds provided to Atlanta University by the Carnegie Foundation. In 1954 Fort Valley State University began receiving general budget funds for continued research at the rate of $10,000 annually.

In 1947 the Prairie View Substation at Prairie View A & M University in Texas was established. From 1963 to 1967 it received $129,676 from the state. During the same period, it received short-term grants from the Welch Foundation, National Institute of Health, Atomic Energy Com-

Table I.1.
Milestone U.S. Legislation Affecting African American
Higher Education Land-Grant System.

Act	Purpose
Morrill Act (1862)	Established colleges of agriculture, home economics, and mechanical arts. Gave each state 30,000 acres of land (for each senator and each of its representative in Congress) to endow colleges.
Hatch Act (1887)	Provided annual grant for agricultural research, establishing experiment stations.
Second Morrill Act (1890)	Established colleges of agriculture, home economics, and mechanical arts for people of color.
Adams Act (1906)	Provided additional funds to each state for agricultural research.
Smith Leaver Act (1914)	Established the Agricultural Extension Service.
Smith Hughes Act (1917)	Established federal support for vocational agriculture in high schools.
Public Law 89-106 (1967)	Provided research funds collectively for 1890 Institutions
Public Law 95-113 (1977)	Made 1890 institutions funding part of the experiment station appropriations.
Gray Amendment (1984)	Authorized Administrator of the Agency for International Development to make available 10 percent of the aggregate funds for activities of economically and socially disadvantaged enterprises to include HBCUs and minority owned private and voluntary organizations.

Source: Mayberry, B.D., ed. *Development of Research at Historically Black Land-Grant Institutions.* Tuskegee, Ala.: The Bicentennial Committee of the Association of Research Directors, 1976.

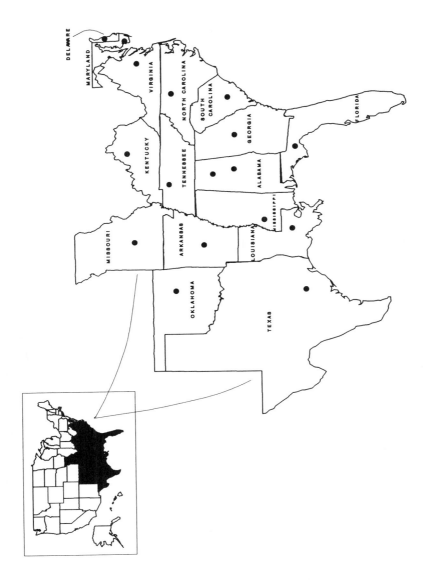

Figure 1. Location of the Seventeen Historically Black (1890) Land-Grant Colleges and Universities.

Table I.2.

Identification of 1890 Land-Grant Institutions, Benchmark Dates on Founding, Program Development and Sponsoring Agency

Institution	Founded	Initiated 4-Year Program	Initiated Graduate Program	Achieved Regional Accreditation	Sponsor
Alabama A & M University	1875	1939	1958	1963	Group of Ex-slaves
Alcorn State University	1871	1871	1975	1961	State Legislature
University of Arkansas— Pine Bluff	1873	1929	a	1933	State Legislature
Delaware State College	1891	1947	a	1957	State Legislature
Florida A & M University	1887	1909	1951	1949	State Legislature
Fort Valley State University	1895	1945	1957	1957	Citizens Group
Kentucky State University	1886	1929	1972	1939	State Legislature
Langston University	1897	1897	a	1939	Territorial Legislature
Lincoln University	1866	1935	1940	1935	Civil War Negro Infantry Men
University of Maryland— Eastern Shore	1886	1936	1978	1953	
North Carolina A & T State University	1891	1925	1939	1936	
Prairie View A & M University	1876	1901	1954	1958	State Legislature
South Carolina State College	1872	1924	1948	1960	State Legislature
Southern University	1880	1922	1957	1958	State Legislature
Tennessee State University	1909	1922	1942	1946	State Legislature
Tuskegee University	1881	1928	1943	1933	State Legislature

mission, and National Science Foundation. During the 1950s, the research program further improved with grants from the Agricultural Research Service—USDA, National Institute of Health, and Atomic Energy Commission.

However, at some 1890 institutions, no sponsored agricultural research existed until 1967. At that time, the black Land-Grant Institutions received, collectively, an allocation of $283,000 under new Public Law 89-106, and from 1967 to 1971 funding for agricultural research continued at the same level as that allocated in 1967. This amount, though small, served to stimulate and encourage research at the institutions. Furthermore, from fiscal year 1972, when Tuskegee University officially became a part of the 1890 Land-Grant System, to the present, funding from the Cooperative State Research Service—USDA, has substantially increased and is now a part of the regular appropriation, rather than a special grant to be renegotiated each year.

Thus, from their humble beginnings with little or no resources, the HBCUs have evolved into a major resource for resident instruction, human resource and rural community development, international development, cooperative extension, and agricultural research. This record is indeed an impressive achievement in the chronicle of higher education in the United States. Three papers in this historical development section of the proceedings highlight the development of the 1890 institutions, as well as the growth and development of agricultural economics and rural development programs within these colleges and universities.

A Contemporary View

This section provides a contemporary assessment of the 1890 Land-Grant Institutions' colleges of agriculture by describing four selected functional areas: resident instruction, research, extension, and international programs. Resident instruction, as was the case with other Land-Grant Institutions, was the first functional program area of colleges of agriculture within 1890 institutions. Although discovery of knowledge and information dissemination are central to the mission of 1890 institutions, formal research and extension programs are relatively recent components. International programs are the most recent of these functional areas, having achieved official recognition and expansion only in the 1970s.

By most measures, the resources allocated to instruction, research, extension, and international program activities at 1890 institutions have been meager compared to those given to 1862 colleges of agriculture. Each of the four papers in Part II discusses competition for resources across these functional areas. Historically, federal sources of funding have provided the larger share of resources to those functional areas of the colleges of agriculture. In fact, the federal government has provided the bulk of the financial support in those instances where state governments have given low priority to their respective 1890 institutions. Furthermore, in recent years the federal government has become a strong advocate of the 1890 Land-Grant System and the HBCUs as part of a strategy to support African American universities until students and clientele can gain equal support from other institutions.

For a number of reasons, the extent to which instruction, research, extension, and international program activities of the 1890 institutions are integrated (or coordinated) with those of 1862 universities in their respective states varies widely. First, some Land-Grant Institutions have acted under court order to coordinate activities in resident instruction programs. Second, federal competitive grant programs, particularly in the international arena, have fostered a climate where incentives are given to institutions (1890 and 1862) whose work demonstrates collaborative activities on projects. Third, economic reasons have required some states to consider the coordination and integration of programs with other groups. For example, at present two 1890 institutions have a majority white student population (Lincoln University and Kentucky State University) and three others (University of Arkansas—Pine Bluff, Delaware State University, and Tennessee State University) have a significant number of nonblack students attending their institutions.

In the unique institutional evolution of the four functional activities— instruction, research, extension, and international programs—the schools have excelled, achieving national and international recognition in each area. Specifically, the instructional programs at the 1890 colleges and universities have had a long-standing reputation for being strong programs. They have accepted students from disadvantaged economic and academic backgrounds and have excelled in preparing these students for competitive performance in the work force, in graduate degree programs, and in professional schools. Furthermore, extension and research programs have developed expertise in contributing to the economic viability of limited-resource farmers. International development projects of 1890 institutions have been able to build on the strength in the other functional areas because of the institutions' reputation for small farms delivery programs in the United States.

While these colleges and universities have had a rich history and have developed a reputation for their teaching, research, extension, and international programs, many more challenges currently await them. The need for additional resources and the need for articulating the mission of the 1890 institutions in a desegregated society are just two of the many important challenges.

Visions of the Future

We have arrived at a point in time when it is appropriate to consider the question: Where should we go from here? After recounting the rich history of the 1890 institutions and assessing their current status, we must now ask such a bold question. Yet in doing so, we must consider the future of these universities and indeed the future of African Americans in both higher education and the larger American society. To do so, it might be useful to reflect for a moment on two intellectual giants who engaged in very passionate and often times bitter debate on educational philosophies and strategies for African Americans: Booker T. Washington, the founder of Tuskegee University, and W.E.B. DuBois, the founder of the NAACP.

History records the philosophical positions of these great men very clearly. Washington advocated vocational education as a strategy for achieving the goals he envisioned for the African American community. In a speech given in Atlanta in September 1885, Washington asked for help to secure better education (vocational) for his people and offered in return his acceptance of racial segregation. Washington stated: "In all things that are purely social we can be as separate as the fingers, yet one as the hand in all things essential to mutual progress."

DuBois challenged this basic philosophy of Washington in *The Souls of Black Folks* (DuBois, 1961). He advocated a philosophy and strategy similar to today's civil rights leaders. It should be noted that while there were substantial differences between the two men's philosophies, similarities also existed. DuBois wrote:

> So far as Mr. Washington preaches Thrift, Patience, and Industrial Training for the masses, we must hold up his hands and strive with him . . . but so far as Mr. Washington apologizes for injustice, North or South, does not rightly value the privilege and duty of voting . . . and opposes the higher training and ambition of our brighter minds—so far as he, the South, or the Nation does this—we must unceasingly and firmly oppose them. (Katz, 1968)

The issues and philosophies articulated in this collection of papers will not likely provide such a sharp contrast in philosophy or strategy. However, to the extent that the authors' perspectives reflect different experiences, they may provide unique visions of the future. Three papers provide this insight into the future directions of 1890 colleges and universities and their roles in helping this nation compete in a global economy.

Informing Institutional Design

Debates regarding the question of institutional design have strong emotional and political implications which have, for the most part, taken place in the courts. Rarely has such a discussion taken place as part of a professional meeting of agricultural scientists and administrators. Here within Part IV of these proceedings, a group of papers present clear, yet opposing prescriptive views on alternative institutional designs and strategies with the goal of providing educational opportunities for the African American. The papers range in position from maintaining the current institutional arrangement of 1890 institutions to merging components of the Land-Grant System.

The final paper provides some specific policy recommendations based on a study conducted by COSBAE. This comprehensive work may, in fact, have even greater applicability to other agricultural professional organizations as they consider methods to increase the number of African American scientists in their respective professions.

References

Bellamy, Donald and Linda M. Ghelfi. "Southern Persistently Low-Income Counties: Social and Economic Characteristics." In *Rural Development Issues of the Nineties: Perspectives From the Social Sciences.* Ed. Thomas T. Williams et al. Tuskegee,

Al.: George Washington Carver Agricultural Experiment Station, Tuskegee University, 1989.

Carter, Deborah J. and Reginald Wilson. "Eighth Annual Status Report Minorities in Higher Education." Washington, D.C.: Office of Minority Concerns, American Council on Education, December 1989.

DuBois, William E.B. *The Souls of Black Folk.* New York: Fawcett Publications, 1961.

Jaynes, Gerald D. and Robin M. Williams, Jr., eds. *A Common Destiny: Blacks and American Society.* Washington, D.C.: National Academy Press, 1989.

Katz, William L. *Eyewitness: The Negro in American History.* New York: Pitman Publishing Company, 1968, p. 349

Litcher, Daniel T. and Tim B. Heaton. "Black Composition and Change in the Nonmetropolitan South." *Rural Sociology* 51, no. 3 (1986), pp. 343–353.

Mayberry, B. D., ed. *Development of Research at Historically Black Land-Grant Institutions.* Tuskegee, Ala.: The Bicentennial Committee of the Association of Research Directors, 1976.

Moen, Jon R. "Poverty in the South." *Economic Review*, Federal Reserve Bank of Atlanta, January/February 1989, pp.36–46.

Sawhill, Isabel V. "Poverty in the U.S.: Why is it so Persistent?" *Journal of Economic Literature* 26 (September 1988), pp. 1073–1119.

Steele, Shelby. "The Recoloring of Campus Life: Student Racism, Academic Pluralism, and the End of a Dream." *Harper's Magazine* (February 1989), pp. 47–55.

U.S. Department of Commerce, Bureau of Census. Poverty in the United States: 1987. Current Population Report, ser. P-60, no. 163. Washington, D.C.: U.S. Government Printing Office, 1989.

Williams, Thomas T. and Handy Williamson, Jr. "Teaching, Research and Extension Programs at Historically Black (1890) Land-Grant Universities." *Southern Journal of Agricultural Economics* 17 (July 1985), pp. 31–41.

PART I

Historical Development of 1890 Institutions

Courtesy of Archives, Horris Burke Frissell Library, Tuskegee University, Tuskegee, Alabama.

1

Land-Grant Institutions:
Their Struggle for Survival and Equality

Fred Humphries

As we approach the centennial celebration of our 1890 land-grant college system, it is essential that we reflect on both the historical developments which have brought us to this point and project into the future to what our institutions can and should be. The following includes an overview of the evolution of land-grant functions in our 1890 institutions, as well as some concepts of what the roles of such institutions should be as we begin the next one hundred years.

The land-grant idea began in 1862 with the passage of the first Morrill Act. The purpose of the act was to democratize higher education by establishing institutions at which

> the leading objective shall be, without excluding other scientific and classical studies and including military tactics, to teach such branches of learning as are related to agricultural and mechanical arts, in such a manner as the legislatures of the states may be respectively prescribed, in order to promote the liberal and practical education of the industrial classes in the several pursuits and professions of life. (Morrill Act, 1862)

However, since the vast majority of blacks were still in slavery when the land-grant idea began, blacks did not profit immediately from the system. With the exception of Alcorn State University in Mississippi, Hampton University in Virginia, and Claflin University in South Carolina, no other black institution received 1862 funds prior to 1890. Kentucky State College eventually received 1862 land-grant funds in

3

1897. Since the first Morrill Act did not divide funds on racial lines, in the vast majority of cases the funds were used to develop white colleges from which black people were excluded.

In the social and political framework of the 1880s—when the worth of black people was being devalued; when disfranchisement was making blacks a powerless people; when white leaders were openly questioning the need for higher education for blacks; and when the Supreme Court decisions, such as the Civil Rights Cases of 1883 and *U.S. v. Cruikshank* in 1876, were eroding most civil rights gains—Congress needed a new initiative to assure land-grant education for black people. So, on August 30, 1890, Congress enacted the second Morrill Act, which provided "a just and equitable division of the funds to be received under this act between one college for white students and one institution for colored students . . . ." (Morrill Act, 1890). The same act also pointed out "that no money shall be paid out under this act to any State or Territory for the support and maintenance of a college where a distinction of race or color is made in the admission of students . . . ." (ibid.). As such, this act made an effort, on one hand, to remove the possibility of inequality or racial discrimination; on the other, it provided that land-grant funds be equitably divided where separate schools of the two races were maintained. Thus, the federal government had given open approval to the "separate-but-equal" philosophy six years before the *Plessy v. Ferguson* decision of 1896.

Within three years after the passage of the second Morrill Act, each of the seventeen states which were maintaining dual systems of schools had officially accepted the provisions of this act. Although some states used existing private institutions to provide land-grant services to their black citizens, by 1897 each of the seventeen states, except Tennessee, had established a state-supported land-grant college. It should be noted that Knoxville College initially held the federal funds for land-grant education for blacks, and Tennessee did not establish a separate black land-grant college until 1912.

Because of the low educational level of blacks, who were only twenty-five years out of slavery, the 1890 institutions began with elementary and secondary students as the largest portion of their enrollment and worked hard to achieve normal school status. For example, as late as 1915 there were but 64 public high schools for blacks in the southern states, and only 45 of them offered a four-year curriculum

(Klein, 1930). In the seventeen states with black land-grant institutions in 1928, there were 12,922 students enrolled in colleges, of which 9,395 (or 73 percent) were in private colleges while only 3,527 (27 percent) were enrolled in black land-grant colleges (ibid.). Thus, it appears black land-grant colleges started out trying to be all things to all people. However, because of the tremendous need, they concentrated primarily on preparing teachers and, therefore, devoted themselves to the traditional curriculum: the classics, letters, humanities, and other aspects of liberal arts. In the early years, agricultural and mechanical arts training were only offered primarily in a practical manner or through a small number of courses in selected areas. The formal curricula in these areas only began emerging after 1900.

During the first two decades of the twentieth century, black land-grant colleges struggled against tremendous odds to establish collegiate programs leading to the bachelor's degree. Inadequate funds and other resources were common threads which ran through each of the colleges, as was the inability of the colleges to attract adequately trained teachers to their staffs. Furthermore, the states provided salaries which were slightly more than half of what white professors with similar training, ability, and experience received. It was not until 1931 that more college students than secondary students were enrolled in the 1890 colleges (Holmes, 1934). Thus, black colleges, unlike their white counterparts, had to spend most of their resources on sub-collegiate level instruction. Yet, despite all of these disadvantages, most of the 1890 colleges were able to develop bona fide four-year, standard college degree programs and to receive accreditation by regional accrediting agencies during the 1930s.

Still, even as late as the 1950s, our 1890 institutions placed emphasis on teacher training. Even though the traditional land-grant areas of agriculture, mechanical arts, and home economics had been well developed, approximately 90 percent of the graduates in these disciplines still prepared to enter the field of teaching. For, unlike their white counterparts, 1890 institutions did not have the resources to train their students to be scientific farmers, research scientists, engineers, and the like, neither were most able to offer official ROTC training until after World War II. As various suits were filed for blacks to gain admission to the graduate programs of white institutions, beginning with *Lloyd Gaines v. University of Missouri* in 1938, graduate programs were hastily set up at black land-grant colleges. Beginning with Prairie View A & M University and Virginia State University in 1937, other 1890 institutions began graduate programs. Some, like Florida A & M University (1953), were elevated to university status and given schools of law, pharmacy, liberal arts, agricultural education, agronomy, home economics, and others. Yet, while new graduate programs were introduced in most 1890 institutions, education at the master's degree level was the most popular major by far.

If 1890 institutions were weak in carrying out their land-grant functions, this can be also traced directly to their inability to receive an equitable share of federal funds due to racial discrimination. At the Conference of Presidents of Negro Land-Grant Colleges in Washington, D.C. in 1935, the black presidents complained to Secretary of Agriculture Henry A. Wallace that in cooperative extension, black colleges received annually $2,800,000 less than they were entitled to, and that in 1933 "not one of the states which support a separate Land-Grant College for Negroes has established an agricultural experiment sub-station in connection with the institution for Negroes" (Davis, 1934:20). In the seventeen states, even though blacks had 23 percent of the population, they received only 6 percent of funds appropriated to those states to support land-grant institutions (ibid.).

As late as the mid-1960s, federal and state aid to the sixteen predominantly black land-grant colleges (West Virginia State College lost its land-grant status in 1957) amounted to approximately $70 million annually, while predominantly white land-grant institutions in the same states received approximately $580 million (Payne, 1970). This same report stated that when federal aid to land-grant schools in the sixteen states was taken separately, predominantly white institutions received eleven times as much as predominantly black institutions. Some of the extreme examples include: the University of Florida, with less than 5 times the enrollment of Florida A & M University, received 24 times as much in federal aid; the University of Georgia, with 10 times the enrollment of Fort Valley State College, received nearly 24 times as much federal aid; and Mississippi State University, which enrolled 4.5 times as many students at Alcorn State University, received almost 14 times as much in federal aid (ibid.). The inequities existed in varying proportions in each of the sixteen states and adversely affected programmatic development and service delivery by historically black land-grant institutions.

In the so-called "formula funds" (Morrill-Nelson, Hatch, Smith-Lever, Bankhead-Jones, etc.), black land-grant institutions fared even worse. The report again said: Formula funds to white land-grant institutions in fiscal year 1967 amounted to $59.3 million as compared to only $1.4 million to Negro land-grant colleges—a ratio of 43 to 1 (ibid.). Reflecting on the plight of these institutions, Earl J. McGrath in *Predominantly Negro Colleges and Universities* (1965) estimated that it would take $125 million in "catch up" funds for black land-grant colleges, and that that amount might be inadequate. It seems fair to say that for the first 77 years of the existence of 1890 institutions, grave inequities in funding prevented the institutions from effectively carrying out the land-grant services that they had been established to deliver.

Beginning in 1967 under Public Law 89-106, the Secretary of the U.S. Department of Agriculture (USDA) allocated $283,000 of discretionary funds for research at the sixteen black land-grant institutions for an average of $17,658 each. In 1972, the agricultural research allocation was increased significantly, and Tuskegee University became eligible to receive these funds. The Food and Agriculture Act of 1977 (PL 95-113) provided permanent or sustained institutional federal funding for black land-grant colleges. Section 1445 of that act—the Evans-Allen Research Program—provided formula-funded programs for 1890 institutions.

Four years later in 1981, this act was amended to provide that not less than six percent of Smith-Lever funds be allocated for extension work at the 1890 institutions. Under Public Law 97-98, Section 1443, Congress authorized $50 million over five years to upgrade agricultural research facilities and equipment at historically black land-grant colleges and universities (Association of Research Directors/CSRS, 1986).

Sustained federal funding has enabled 1890 institutions to develop long-range and well-designed research programs which have contributed significantly to local communities, to their states, and to the nation. Furthermore, it has brought these historically black institutions into the mainstream of the nation's agricultural research system and has motivated our research scientists to take leadership roles in building human capital and in developing food and fiber for the world.

Although time will not permit a discussion of the types and quality of research completed by the 1890 schools, the book *Development of Research at Historically Black Land-Grant Institutions* (Mayberry, et al., 1976) has summarized this information. This volume reveals that in making plans for long-term research, 1890 institutions and Tuskegee University considered several factors of utmost importance: (1) national priority research needs, (2) local and state research needs, and (3) availability of essential resources including money, qualified and interested personnel, facilities, and accessories (ibid.). The major areas in which research activities took place were: (1) animal science, (2) natural resources, (3) human nutrition, (4) plant soil, and (5) rural development. Under these five categories and during the first nine years of CSRS funding, 234 research projects under 87 research programs were completed or were still in progress by 1976 (ibid.).

Thus, after having virtually been denied direct funding for research and extension service during the 77 years after the enactment of the second Morrill Act, the 1890 institutions took the meager appropriations and demonstrated to several states, the nation, and the world that they are capable of doing quality research and rendering outstanding extension services that contribute significantly to the uplifting of humankind everywhere.

Since 1967, federal government support for 1890 institutions has grown at a tremendous rate. While it may not have been as fast as administrators of those institutions would have desired, we cannot overlook the increase from $283,000 in 1967 to over $25 million in 1989 in CSRS research funds alone. Despite the fact that some of our institutions lost all or most of their agricultural programs due to the integration/desegregation decision, these and other federal funds have enabled 1890 institutions to fulfill many of the land-grant functions which led to their establishment one hundred years ago.

With the advent of sustained federal funding, 1890 institutions have ventured into areas of research and extension that they would never have dreamed of just thirty years ago. An agricultural engineer at Fort Valley State College invented and patented an ice-walled container for the storage of leafy vegetables; Delaware State College points with pride to its evaluation of culinary herbs and essential oil plants as cash crops in its state; the University of Arkansas at Pine Bluff has taken the leadership throughout the state in the growing field of aquaculture;

Florida A & M University has won acclaim with its research program in aquatic insects, especially mayflies; Alcorn State University has blazed the trail with its feeder pig productivity project for low-income rural dwellers in Southwest Mississippi; Kentucky State University and Lincoln University have been demonstrating the value of urban gardening, while Prairie View A & M University has been leading the way with its International Dairy Goat Research Center (Neyland, 1989). The above are only a few examples of research and extension services at 1890 institutions.

However, the advances in research and extension work at 1890 institutions, made possible by federal funds, have been offset by the failure of states to provide matching dollars for research— something the states have historically done for 1862 institutions. Since many of these limited-resource farmers are black, it raises disturbing questions of racial discrimination. Lack of funds at 1890 institutions has hampered efforts to remedy many of the problems faced by limited-resource farmers and rural people, and since many of these farmers are black, it raises disturbing questions of racial discrimination. In fact, a case can be made for the loss of black farms and black farmers leaving the South or remaining in poverty because, year after year, 1890 institutions were not given matching dollars to help design research and extension services to meet the needs of rural, limited-resource people. Now, however, throughout the South, 1890 institutions are giving major emphasis to agricultural research and extension services designed to explore and deliver much needed technical and educational assistance to the poor, underprivileged, undereducated, unemployed, politically powerless people in the states and areas they serve. Yet, common problems still continue: high rates of illiteracy, teenage pregnancy, malnutrition, infant mortality, crime, drugs, and other disabilities associated with poverty level existence.

Although 1890 institutions do not receive the necessary matching dollars for federal funds from the states and thus do not have the resources to deliver the quality of service that their constituents need, being historically black institutions and steeped in the land-grant tradition, they have the know-how among the faculty and research scientists, the compassion, the desire and the professional attitude to render services to "help people help themselves."

If, however, a bright future for 1890 institutions is to be realized, then state support in the form of matching funds with additional dollars to show a commitment to these quality programs is absolutely essential. Programs such as agriculture and natural resources, community resource development, family and economic well-being, 4-H youth development, and others must be given ample research and extension services. States must realize that 1890 institutions are prepared to deliver services that impact rural housing, rural revitalization, limited-resource farmers with 1 to 50 acres of land and gross sales of $10,000-$20,000 per year, and other limited-resource clientele. These groups require intensive educational efforts, close supervision, and continuous follow-up activity. These services are expensive in terms of both human and fiscal resources.

At a time when increased federal funds are being directed toward 1890 institutions, the very existence, in most states, of such institutions is being challenged by threats of abolition or of merger from conservative or reactionary political groups who have rejected equality for black institutions. In *Adams v. Richardson*, commonly called *Adams* States Case, the federal court compelled ten southern states to establish unitary systems of higher education and to present "acceptable and adequate desegregation plans." Judge John R. Pratt maintained that "the desegregation process should take into account the unequal status of black colleges and the real danger that desegregation will diminish higher educational opportunities of Blacks . . . ." He further emphasized that all plans for establishing a unitary system of higher education in the several states must "enhance" black institutions and that the implementation of a desegregation plan "may not place a greater burden" upon such institutions (Neyland, 1987:18–44). The result of this decision, along with other initiatives, has been the loss of programs and services at 1890 institutions; however, in most cases they have had the broad-based effect of increasing academic offerings, horizontally and vertically.

So today, 1890 institutions stand firmly as major comprehensive colleges and universities in their respective states, offering strong baccalaureate and master's degree programs in such fields as business, computer science, engineering, journalism, natural sciences, technology, architecture, agribusiness, the liberal arts, and a host of other sound academic, scientific, and technological programs.

Now, in addition to the more than 900 baccalaureate and 226 master's degree programs in the 1890 land-grant institutions and at Tuskegee, six of these institutions offer one or more programs leading to the doctorate in such fields as pharmaceutical sciences, physics, special education, school administration and supervision, veterinary medicine, food science, plant and soil science, and others (Smith, 1990:12–16). The curriculum offering of the 1890 institutions is on a par with any group of comprehensive institutions in this country with similar missions. They are accredited by the major accrediting agencies throughout the nation, and, in almost every case, faculties hold terminal degrees from some of the most prestigious institutions in the nation. Annually they produce a disproportionately large share of the baccalaureate degree holders in the nation.

The future for these institutions is bright. Recently, the 1890 Capacity Building Program, designed to improve the quality of resident instruction, was enacted by Congress to set up centers of excellence and to support selected areas of research. This program appears to be a prime opportunity for 1890 institutions to further enrich their programs and extend their services. State matching funds are, however, essential for participation in the federal Capacity Building Program. With both matching and commitment funds, our institutions can expand their programs at the graduate level to provide training for agricultural teachers and scientists who will be able to perform effectively in the classroom, in high technology areas, and on the international scene, as well as to meet the various demands for their services by their limited-resource, rural clientele.

Despite limited resources, the future for 1890 institutions is bright. They are able to garner more and more research dollars. They are poised to meet head-on one of the greatest challenges facing this nation: educating greater numbers of black students. With appropriate support at the state and federal levels, they will play a major role in solving the problem of underrepresented black talent. Hopefully, the importance of the 1890 institutions will be recognized and supported and in the halls of state legislatures and in the U.S. Congress. For, with adequate support, the future is unlimited. Without an equitable share of both state and federal support, however, 1890 institutions cannot fully realize their mission and may thus be condemned to an uncertain or mediocre uncertain existence as they begin their second century of service.

References

Association of Research Directors, Cooperative State Research Services. "Progress and Productivity Through Research and Service: Agricultural Research at the 1890 Institutions," Washington, D.C.: U.S. Department of Agriculture, 1986.

Davis, J.W. *Land-Grant Colleges for Negroes.* Institute, W. Va.: West Virginia State College Bulletin. Series 321, no. 5, 1934.

Holmes, D.O.W. *The Evolution of the Negro College.* New York: Columbia University Teachers College, 1934.

Mayberry, B.D., ed. *Development of Research at Historically Black Land-Grant Institutions.* Tuskegee, Ala.: The Bicentennial Committee of the Association of Research Directors, 1976.

Neyland, Leedell W. "Research in 1890 Institutions Since 1967." Unpublished manuscript, 1989.

———. *Florida Agricultural and Mechanical University: A Centennial History 1887–1987.* Tallahassee: FAMU (Florida Agricultural and Mechanical University) Foundation, Inc., 1987.

Payne, W. "The Negro Land-Grant Colleges." *Civil Rights Digest* 1970, p. 12–17.

Smith, James W. "Institutional Programs at Historically Black Land-Grant Institutions." Unpublished manuscript. Virginia State University, Petersburg, Va., 1990.

2

A National Resource—A National Challenge: The 1890 Land-Grant Colleges and Universities

William P. Hytche

As we embark on the celebration of the one hundredth anniversary of the Second Morrill Act of 1890, I feel a particular kinship with Morrill's quest for a truer expression of the American educational ideal. Moving into our second century, we must be as persistent in the protection and development of the 1890 Land-Grant Colleges and Universities as Morrill was in his thirty-year battle to make these very institutions a reality.

Through the years we have been meeting the educational demands of blacks in America as well as research demands of developing nations and rural America. These institutions have proved to be a national resource fervently striving to meet national challenges.

The Second Morrill Act: A Crisis Averted

In the early 1800s, higher education was restricted primarily to classical and theological studies taught within a theoretical context. During the mid-1800s, there was a major reform movement toward a more democratic and utilitarian quality of education focusing on the practical application of physical and natural sciences for the production of skilled farmers and factory workers. Educational concepts covered a broad spectrum of disciplines, and schools were created to advance agriculture, industrial and mechanical arts, and trade. The underlying theme was that agriculture and science should be essential elements in the curriculum complemented by mechanical arts to improve speed and efficiency.

Prior to 1860, higher education was strongly elitist with no access for members of working-class families. This situation moved legislators to establish universities for the rest of society, which ultimately led to the passage of the First Morrill Land-Grant Act of 1862. The primary tenet of the Morrill Act of 1862 was that all Americans should have equal access to higher education and occupations in agriculture and the industrial and mechanical arts. The Morrill Act promoted the philosophy that citizens, regardless of social and economic class, should be afforded the opportunity to achieve according to their own abilities and desires.

In 1865, however, there was a tremendous crisis in the American education system and the land-grant movement. With the emancipation of slaves came the unleashing of a potential work force of 4 million blacks who were primarily illiterate and dysfunctional in a rapidly changing economic climate. Despite dramatic changes in the economy and the emergence of an unsettling era of political chaos, the nation showed little interest in support of equal educational opportunities. Although there were compelling and practical reasons for the nation to invest in equality of opportunity, conservatism prevailed and segregation was reinforced. Entrenched resistance from local and state governments prohibited schools and higher education institutions from receiving resources essential to creating opportunities, while federal laws sanctioned the separate-but-equal doctrine. These laws were embedded in the social fabric of American higher education.

Although unintentional, a significant crisis in American education was averted when Congress enacted the Second Morrill Act in 1890. It was unintentional because the states viewed the legislation as an opportunity to obtain additional funding for 1862 Land-Grant Colleges and Universities. Nevertheless, Congress, in its wisdom, recognized the importance of a national investment in expanding access to neglected segments of the population during a period that was symbolized as Reconstruction.

While the Industrial Revolution was taking shape and powerful forces for educational reform were being generated, Congress, in the Justin

Smith Morrill Act of 1890, set a precedent with the stipulation that black Americans be included in the mainstream of the U.S. educational system. Southern and border states opposed this inclusion and chose to exercise an option provided in the Act by creating separate institutions for blacks—"and you know the rest of the story."

Consequently, today we pay tribute to the foresight and wisdom of Justin Smith Morrill. One hundred years ago, he inspired his congressional colleagues to enfranchise black Americans by making higher educational opportunities accessible to former slaves via these prestigious 1890 Land-Grant Colleges and Universities.

The Early Struggle

Seventeen states, including West Virginia, agreed to establish separate institutions for blacks. Prior to 1890, however, black schools had been founded in 12 of these states, and these were awarded land-grant status. Between 1891 and 1909, the remaining 5 states created black land-grant colleges or universities. Much later, West Virginia rescinded its land-grant university status while Tuskegee Institute (now Tuskegee University) was afforded all the privileges stipulated in the 1890 Act. Today, there are 17 of these 1890 Land-Grant Colleges and Universities located in 16 states.

Despite the absence of land and fiscal support comparable to their 1862 counterparts, these institutions pursued research, teaching, and public service activities through a sustained struggle for racial equality and opportunity.

Blacks in the Early Years

In the early years the struggle to rise from slavery, and the need for black teachers to provide basic skills, training, and primary education, required that normal schools or colleges assume responsibility for the training of teachers in education, agriculture, home economics, and industrial arts. Progress occurred in spite of the absence of basic resources, and new standards of excellence significantly broadened opportunities for black Americans in other sectors of the nation.

The first black college or university to be designated as a land-grant college was Alcorn State University, which was founded in 1871. Its land-grant status was granted under the aegis of the First Morrill Act of 1862. However, it was not so designated by the Mississippi Legislature until 1878.

The period of the 1870s through the 1890s was very lean. Many notable examples of courage and determination chronicle the efforts to educate black people. At what is now Alabama A & M University, for example, founded in 1875 by William Hooper Councill, the annual state appropriation of $4,000 was inadequate to support the institution; therefore, President Councill and his entire faculty contributed their salaries to keep the school open.

During this period, one of Councill's contemporaries, Booker T. Washington, founded Tuskegee Normal and Industrial Institute in 1881 and became the primary fund-raiser among northern philanthropists contributing to black colleges. As the inscription on his monument on the campus at Tuskegee University states, "He lifted the veil of ignorance from his people and pointed the way to progress through education and industry."

A greater pioneer in scientific research during the early years was George Washington Carver, who in 1896 founded the first agricultural experiment station at a predominantly black university. Carver became famous for his ground-breaking research on peanuts, sweet potatoes, soybeans, and cowpeas. It is rather remarkable to note that we are still conducting research on these crops, which speaks to the progressive nature of agricultural science. Carver's research was dedicated to the improvement of nutrition for tenant farm families. His guiding principle was the enhancement of the quality of life, a philosophy which has become the motto of the 1890 community.

Thus, Carver became a living example of "the practical application of science to the wants and welfare of man." Councill, Washington, Carver, and many more black leaders broadened the national consensus for economic well-being through education. These dreams and desires have been eloquently captured in the missions of 1890 institutions and in the hearts and minds of those who have benefitted from this revolutionary investment in democracy.

The 1890 Land-Grant Universities have played a major role in the formation of the land-grant movement. They pioneered resident instruction programs, conducted landmark research, and extended their benefits to the people of rural and neglected communities. The latter was advanced by Thomas M. Campbell, who was inspired by Booker T. Washington to conduct agricultural demonstration programs in rural Alabama.

The frontiers of knowledge and the improvement of the quality of life even permeated international territories early in the development of the black land-grant system. In 1899, students and faculty of Tuskegee, under the leadership of Carver, participated in cotton production research in Togo, West Africa.

A distinguished record of teaching, research, and public service symbolizes the legacy of 1890 Land-Grant Colleges and Universities—a legacy that is inextricably linked to the prominence of such leaders as Horace Mann Bond, Mary McCloud-Bethune, John Hope Franklin, Benjamin Mays, Charles Drew, Charles Turner, Frederick D. Patterson, Walter Massey, Esther Hopkins, Percy Julian, and Carter G. Woodson, to name a few. These visionaries continue to inspire our institutions to pursue excellence while promoting full equality of opportunity.

A National Resource

During the 1950s and 1960s, the escalation of the Civil Rights Movement brought about tremendous pressures to desegregate public systems of education. Desegregation litigation that was originally heard in 1849 was brought before the U.S. Supreme Court under the infamous Plessy Doctrine, while violations of the Fourteenth Amendment were being challenged in South Carolina, Virginia, Delaware, and other states. The question of the constitutionality of separate-but-equal public education dominated the nation's social agenda for more than a decade.

Black primary education withstood the pressure to desegregate, but many black secondary schools became junior high schools, and black colleges were faced with threats of mergers or closure. These challenges forced the land-grant community to mobilize resources to preserve their tradition of excellence and to continue toward the development of competitive academic programs. During these periods of political turbulence, public awareness of the role and contributions of black higher education reached a new high. The historical record of black achievements in higher education provided the most plausible argument for support of Historically Black Colleges and Universities. The unique character of black land-grant colleges and universities contributed to the creation of academic and social programs that enriched the educational and cultural experience for black and multiethnic student bodies.

One of the great strengths of the black land-grant system lies in our academic richness and diversity. During the 1970s, approximately 20 percent of the students enrolled in agriculture at the 1890 Land-Grant Colleges and Universities were nonblack, while 5 percent of the students enrolled in agriculture at 1862 Land-Grant Colleges and Universities were nonwhite. Today, the 1890 Land-Grant Colleges and Universities continue to be the primary source of minority graduates in the agricultural sciences. Our institutions enroll approximately 35 percent of all minorities enrolled in agriculture, but graduate approximately 65 percent of black recipients of bachelor's degrees in agricultural sciences.

Current trends suggest that the 1890 Land-Grant Colleges and Universities will continue to be the primary source of black undergraduate students in agriculture, given the renewed interest and commitment to the survival of black colleges and universities. Economic and social exigencies, local and national, demand that our institutions offer the brilliant and the not so brilliant an opportunity to engage in the extraordinary experience of higher learning. Our students reflect the economic and social conditions of black America. It is within this context that we tailor our enrichment and cultural programs. Our students come from less affluent backgrounds, require substantial financial assistance, and yet demonstrate a strong desire to transcend the limited boundaries of poverty and social neglect. Thus, we must continue to recognize these institutions as vital national resources. This recognition was fostered in 1965 through the efforts of Secretary of Agriculture Clifford M. Hardin, Dr. R. D. Morrison, Dr. C. A. Williams, and others who challenged the nation to come to grips with the failure to build on the highest ideals of the land-grant philosophy.

Consequently, Public Law 89-106, enacted in 1965, gave the U.S. Department of Agriculture (USDA) the legal and political flexibility to fund research at our colleges and universities. We received our first funding in 1967, and this was followed by extension funding in 1977. This funding forged a great partnership between the USDA and the 1890 Land-Grant Colleges and Universities.

A National Challenge

The decade of the 1980s created significant new challenges for higher education and particularly for our Land-Grant Colleges and Universities. There were attempts to dismantle programs and dilute the land-grant mission. Some challenged our existence, while others questioned the relevancy and value of our academic programs. The public and the land-grant community became very concerned about the decline and devaluation of our undergraduate programs. One could almost equate the political tension that emerged with the evolutionary land-grant movement of the 1860s. The debate centered on the following:

- restoring integrity to undergraduate curricula
- creating more relevant academic programs to meet the needs of the agricultural industry and society in general
- maintaining our scientific expertise
- maintaining our worldwide competitive edge in agricultural research and development

This new debate, however, differs from the debate of the 1860s and 1890s in that it was more vociferous and intellectual and had greater economic implications. One school of thought is that we have become so agriculturally efficient that we have researched ourselves out of business. The efficiency of production has led to a farm crisis of such national magnitude that agriculture or a career in the field has been relegated to the lowest level of options among our youth.

It is ironic that the arguments of one hundred years ago are being echoed today. The mission of the land-grant universities a century ago was: to educate people for the purposes of stimulating agricultural production, improving the quality of life, and revitalizing rural America, while producing better citizens in urban, as well as rural, America.

Today we are still attempting to revitalize rural America and motivate our youth to be better citizens. We have not conquered the problems of rural-to-urban migration; the great gulf between the haves and have-nots continues to widen; and the severe problems of crime, drug abuse, teenage pregnancy, poverty, and declining employment prevail. Is our continuing struggle with the problems of one hundred years ago an indictment of our land-grant system? Have we failed to address the "people" problems that were behind the philosophy and intent of Justin Smith Morrill and his colleagues?

To both questions, I would emphatically respond—"No." Although the problems are complex and systemic, we must continue to strengthen our ability to *nurture* the minds and lives of the people we serve. The story of the black land-grant system is the story of ideals and industry— we use a mere 3 percent of our labor force to produce the nation's total food supply; we are the best-fed nation in the world; we export a significant amount of our produce; we are the number one industry in sustaining the world economy; and we are the premier leader in agricultural research. There are skeptics who still regard the land-grant system as a misnomer and agriculture as a mechanic avocation. We must raise public awareness about the critical role that agriculture plays in feeding the nation and in developing the wealth of our natural resources. We must also sound the alarm that it is time for agriculture to turn its sights to future generations.

The Next Century

As we celebrate our centennial, we must look beyond the past and compound our strengths while creating boundless opportunities to surpass the collective history of the land-grant movement. Our future lies in the preservation of our natural resources and the educational development of our human resources. As Abraham Lincoln said, "Upon the subject of education, I can only say that I view it as the most important subject that we as a people can be engaged in."

As we approach the twenty-first century, let us review our distinctive land-grant commitment to scientific research, innovative teaching, and extension services to meet the agricultural needs of the world. This commitment will, however, create new demands for substantial national investments in the land-grant system. It will also create new tensions in public policy and governance issues. This is a challenge that cannot be overlooked as we approach a new era.

As we attempt to focus more on issues and concerns of people, society will demand a greater stake in determining how we address critical issues. Within the coming century several factors must be addressed.

First, the role of agriculture in higher education must be clearly defined. Currently, some believe that the term agriculture is all-encompassing. Others tend to link agriculture and natural resources. Still others tie agriculture to the life sciences, and some groups relate agriculture, forestry, and home economics. Perhaps the definition of agriculture should be reexamined. One should look at agriculture holistically as involving the following:

- the land and its natural resources,
- the production and management of food and fiber; the processing, marketing, and distribution of our food and fiber, and
- the economics and policies involved in all of the above.

Agriculture in the system of higher education should be geared toward developing human resources in all three areas.

Second, human capital must be properly deployed. During the next century there will be a significant shift in the mix of students. Projected increases in enrollment will come primarily from minority groups. Reports indicate that by the year 2001, the majority of students attending college in California and Texas will be Hispanics and blacks. Our institutions must lead the challenge of educating these groups, who, if not trained and provided adequate access to meaningful career opportunities, will diminish significantly the scientific and technical capabilities of the U.S. work force. The agricultural community must also be able to refocus its attention and provide educational opportunities for the increasing number of second-career workers who will require new skills.

To be competitive we must assume a more assertive role in creating meaningful programs for working mothers who are now primary providers of family income. This new clientele will require the creation of new support systems. There is serious concern about the importance of raising admission standards at a time when higher education must respond to the growing underclass. As we raise our standards and entrance requirements, are we excluding a critical segment of our society and denigrating the great American dream which promises equal opportunity for all?

Agriculture must be prepared to be competitive in the marketplace. In order to survive, colleges of agriculture will have to market themselves attractively with creative approaches, such as providing high school partnership programs to improve transition, developing early freshman intervention programs, encouraging retention of students perceived to be at risk, providing substantive academic advice, strengthening student support services, and establishing special tutorial and enrichment programs.

The great challenge of the coming century is that America must find methods of developing and using the varied potential of this diverse population.

Students are the nation's future and must be granted access if we intend to thrive in the twenty-first century and beyond. The social and economic state of black America and the nation compel us to make a radical shift in the business of educating future generations. Declining participation of blacks in higher education and the disproportionate underrepresentation of blacks in the physical, chemical, and biological sciences demand a bold substantial response from the land-grant community. In 1984–1985, only 3.4 percent of all doctorate recipients in the nation were black in contrast to 74.1 percent who were white Americans. As highlighted in *One-Third of a Nation* (American Council on Education, 1988), in computer sciences only 1 black received a doctorate out of 355 awarded in 1986. In mathematics, blacks received only 6 of the 730 doctorates awarded that same year.

Also in 1986, 89 blacks earned doctorates in the sciences and 14 in engineering. Even worse, in the agricultural sciences black Americans represent fewer than 0.25 percent of all master's degrees and fewer than 1.5 percent of doctorates. These data are compelling in a society that is losing its competitive edge in domestic and international markets because we are unwilling to use the richness, creativity, and diversity of the nation's land-grant systems.

Building partnerships is an important element in increasing the number of black Americans in the agricultural sciences. Black land-grant colleges and universities must become a dynamic new force in higher education—a force that future generations need, that the USDA needs, and that the nation needs.

Finally, we must realistically address two other societal issues facing agriculture as we enter the next century: food safety and the environment.

Food Safety

During the next century, the American people will increase the demand for a risk-free society. Food contaminants, bio-hazards, insecticides, and animal growth hormones will be severely restricted; the importance of banning products in the absence of expensive research will be heightened. Agriculture will be forced to change production practices by reducing chemical or hormonal usage, though they are economically sound.

Biotechnology, the buzzword of academia and agroindustry, will continue to flourish, but who will pay the price? Already there are visible signs of resistance from those who doubt the safety and efficacy of biotechnologically produced materials. The conflict of social-vs-health-vs-ethical-vs-economic implications of biotechnology must be resolved by the academic community in partnership with the federal and business sectors. Furthermore, the nation's preeminence in science and technology is being challenged; the land-grant community must maintain its leadership in technology by producing a scientifically literate society at every level of the economy from food vendors to Wall Street economists. The academy must take leadership.

The Environment

Environmental issues surfaced more than a decade ago. Agriculture recognized the need to address critical issues and proposed such initiatives as soil and water conservation, alternative agriculture, and natural resource management. But again, we became bogged down with policy issues rather than appropriate research and technological innovations to effect change.

Agriculture and the land-grant community must be more assertive and public in proclaiming their virtues. For many years, the 1890 Land-Grant Colleges and Universities remained silent partners in agriculture. Today, we are improving our faculty, conducting research for the future, publishing a greater number of papers, interacting with Congress, and assertively marketing our programs. The policymakers and USDA have responded positively.

Through the efforts of a task force created by the Secretary of Agriculture and made up of top-level USDA career appointees, several initiatives crucial to promoting excellence in the agricultural sciences are being undertaken. These include 1890 capacity building, co-locating facilities on our campuses, providing opportunities for exchange of our facilities with USDA agencies, and providing students with work experiences through internships and cooperative education.

The land-grant community must be better prepared to address the problems of global climate change, organic depletion, deforestation, and acid rain.

During the next century, the issue of animal welfare will become inextricably tied to environmental issues as animal rights activists gain greater public support. Rather than anticipate their actions, let us embark on a massive educational campaign to heighten public awareness about the use of animals in research. Inform our young people through seminars, publications, and the media that animals can be properly cared for in controlled environments.

A Commitment to the Future

The key element, as we ponder the future, will be leadership. As leaders of the land-grant movement, we will be challenged by politically aware students, a demanding faculty, and a public that will question the yield on their investment in tax dollars. We, as administrators, cannot shun our responsibilities or minimize the role of students, faculty, and the public. We have been charged with the responsibility of challenging students and faculty to achieve excellence. The future will demand that universities explore a range of possibilities for improving instruction, evaluating the tracking process, and creating a wider selection of flexible educational opportunities. Faculty will not acquire stature simply because of their pioneering research, but because they are great artists whose art is conveyed through the transmission of knowledge.

Research will have its place but not at the expense of creating intellectual tension in the classroom. Given the influx of an ethnically different mix of students, we must strongly support equality of opportunity through the achievement of excellence. As more minorities enter our institutions, they will demand integrity in the academic program. A grade of "A" will have to be validated based on student and faculty performance. An "A" must stand for achievement and performance in the classroom, library, or laboratory. Higher education is a place where great minds engage in democratic social relationships unaffected by ethnic and economic differences. Thus, higher education should transform students intellectually and socially.

Students should emerge from higher education with an understanding of both individual rights and responsibilities and with some perspective of the human role in God's universe. The challenge to gain sound values is beautifully worded in a *Miami Herald* newspaper headline of several months ago. "Moral citizens aren't born; they're educated." I challenge you to assist students in becoming critically aligned with democratic principles and values that can elevate people beyond any social malaise of the world.

Let me address specifically the 1890 community for a moment. As we approach the twenty-first century, we will undergo constant curriculum revitalization. Our 1890 universities cannot afford the luxury of becoming so highly specialized that we forget our history. However, our history alone will not guarantee our future survival. Specifically, I can see our agriculture curricula in the twenty-first century focusing on six areas.

- **Scientific literacy and competencies**. Graduates must be competent in the agricultural, physical, or biological sciences at the highest level of academic achievement.

- **Communication**. Our graduates must be able to communicate effectively in written, oral, and graphic forms.

- **Appreciation and comprehension**. Students must be firmly grounded in the arts, humanities, and the social and behavioral sciences.

- **Economics and business principles**. Students must become more competent in business and economics. Agribusiness continues to be one of our most attractive academic areas, and this trend is expected to continue.

- **Global awareness**. Students must have an appreciation of our world interdependence. They must become more aware of the impact of agriculture on world society. The need for foreign language competency is crucial.

- **And finally, thinking**. Our curriculum must encourage the development of lifelong skills. Students must become competent in problem-solving, reasoning, synthesis, logic, leadership, and management. The latter is crucial in an ever-increasing information age.

We must expand our pool of academically qualified minorities. Let us be realistic and recognize that pressures exerted on majority institutions to recruit more minorities will escalate and, given the abundance of financial resources, the competition will be fierce. Given greater gender and racial diversity, we must establish innovative instructional support systems and engage in careful review, exhaustive planning, and focused implementation of our academic mission. In assuring the reality of our academic mission we must:

- motivate faculty to be more sensitive to the needs of special students and to align teaching styles with learning styles,

- develop leadership and broaden future generations' knowledge devoid of arrogance and elitism, and

- create incentives and rewards for faculty who demonstrate a commitment to academic excellence and institutional change.

The century-old question will not go away in the twenty-first century. Our critics will continue to ask why we need 1890 Land-Grant Colleges and Universities. Our answer now and through the twenty-first century must be "demonstrated excellence without excuse." When asked, "Why black colleges?", I say to you, be on the offensive and say, "Are Catholics asked, 'Why Notre Dame?' Are Jews asked, 'Why Brandeis?'" These institutions enrich the academy, broaden the nation's intellectual resources, and foster the highest ideals of a democratic society.

I hope I have been able to affirm your belief in the interrelationships of our programs and the importance of agriculture and the land-grant movement in the years ahead. Let us all work together to enhance the image of agriculture and our research capability and to increase the size and diversity of our minority expertise in the agricultural sciences. Our institutions remain confident and committed to the vigor and value of the 1890 mission as essential to our historical identity. Our history of emancipation has created extraordinary opportunities to transform the lives of millions of young men and women who may have languished unchallenged, unrevealed, and possibly shattered by an impersonal society. We must continue to magnify our history and build on our success as social equalizers of the world.

Permission to publish the Justin Smith Morrill Memorial Lecture has been granted by author and Cooperative State Research Service, USDA. This paper was presented in Washington, D.C., November 20, 1989.

References

American Council on Education, Education Commission of the States. *One-Third of a Nation: A Report of the Commission on Minority Participation in Education and American Life.* Washington, D.C.: American Council on Education, May, 1988.

Cobb, H. E. "A Perspective on the Status and Prospects of the Public Black College." Unpublished paper, Southern University, Baton Rouge, La., n.d.

Mayberry, B.D., ed. *Development of Research at Historically Black Land-Grant Institutions.* Tuskegee, Ala.: The Bicentennial Committee of the Association of Research Directors, 1976.

Monsanto Company. *Of the Earth: Agriculture and the New Biology.* Monsanto Company, St. Louis, Missouri, n.d.

National Association of State Universities and Land-Grant Colleges. *Serving the World, The People and Ideas of America's State and Land-Grant Universities.* Washington, D.C.: National Association of State Universities and Land-Grant Colleges, 1987.

Rasmussen, W. D. *Taking the University to the People.* Ames, Iowa: Iowa State University Press, 1989.

Schor, Joel. *Agriculture in the Black Land-Grant System to 1930.* Talahassee, Fl.: Florida A&M University Press, 1981.

U.S. Department of Agriculture. Science and Education Administration. "Review of the Bankhead-Jones Program: Final Report." Washington, D.C.: U.S. Department of Agriculture, August, 1980.

Williams, Thomas T. *The Unique Resources of the 1890 Land-Grant Institutions and Implications for International Development.* Baton Rouge, Louisiana: Louisiana State University Printing Office, 1979.

Wilson, Edward, et al. *Strengthening 1890 Land-Grant Institutions.* Report to the U.S. Department of Agriculture, Lincoln University, Jefferson City, Mo., 1980.

Wojcik, J. *The Arguments of Agriculture.* West Lafayette, Ind.: Purdue University Press, 1989.

Wright, Chester Wilbert. *A History of the Black Land-Grant Colleges 1890-1916.* Ann Arbor, Mich.: University Microfilms International, 1981.

3

Development of Agricultural Economic Programs at the 1890 Land-Grant Institutions

Sidney H. Evans, Donald R. McDowell,
and Ridgely A. Mu' Min

Introduction

Agricultural economics, as a field of study may be defined as a branch of applied economics, which consists of the application of economic techniques and ways of thinking to agricultural and rural activities (*International Encyclopedia of Education*, 1987). The field may be divided broadly into (1) agricultural production, including farm management; (2) supply, demand, and prices, marketing and distribution and international trade in relation to agricultural products; (3) and agricultural policy, including location of production, land use, agrarian reform, rural and community development, and finance and credit (ibid.).

The history of the discipline had its auspicious beginning in the late 1800s and early 1900s. Formal education in agricultural economics began in Germany and the United States in the latter part of the nineteenth century. Courses were listed at Cornell University and the University of Illinois in 1868. In England formal teaching in the subject began at the University of Cambridge in 1896 (ibid.).

In the United States, the agricultural depression of the 1890s led to intensification of study, and in the early years of the twentieth century an independent tradition of agricultural economics was taking shape, influenced particularly by R. T. Ely, T. N. Carver, E. G. Nourse and H. C. Taylor, and later by C. F. Warren, and J. D. Black (ibid.). Foremost among the early economic theorists was Professor Henry C. Taylor, noted as the first professor of agricultural economics in a Land-Grant Institution, the author of the first American textbook dealing with the principles of agricultural economics, and the organizer and first Chief of the Bureau of Agricultural Economics in the U. S. Department of Agriculture (Taylor, 1952). Taylor first taught a course in agricultural economics during the school year 1902–1903 while at the University of Wisconsin.

T. N. Carver is recorded as teaching the first courses in agricultural economics at the University of Wisconsin and Harvard. Since its early existence the discipline is now taught at almost all, if not all, Land-Grant Institutions. Moreover, today, agricultural economists are included in the teaching, research, and extension service staffs of all the land-grant colleges and universities are found throughout the numerous and far-flung agencies of the U. S. Department of Agriculture (USDA). They are also included on the staffs of many privately supported universities and research foundations as well as the great trade concerns and corporations which pride themselves on being the embodiment of practical American business skill (ibid.).

These land-grant colleges and universities, established under the Morrill Act of 1862, were initially given 30,000 acres of federally owned land for each senator and representative. Proceeds from sale of this land were to have been used "to provide colleges for the benefit of agriculture and the mechanical arts." As of today, seventy-two land-grant colleges and universities have been established. These institutions have been divided into two diversified institutions: the 1862 Land-Grant Institutions, which are predominantly white, and the 1890 institutions, which are predominately black. Each Land-Grant Institution has its own unique history.

In light of the centennial of the 1890 institutions, the general objectives of this paper are to give some insight on the development, existence, and status of agricultural economics programs at the 1890 Land-Grant Institutions. We also outline the chronological evolution of one of the 1890 institutions.

Historical Development of 1890 Institutions

On July 2, 1862, President Lincoln signed into law a bill introduced by Congressman Justin Morrill of Vermont to establish land-grant universities. The intent of this legislation, formally entitled the Morrill Act of 1862, was to establish a Land-Grant Institution in each state to educate citizens in the fields of agriculture, home economics, the mechanical arts, and other useful professions. In addition, land-grant universities were to generate new knowledge, apply it to problems of society, and extend that knowledge to others beyond academia (Schuh, 1986). It was a tripartite mission: teaching, research and extension (ibid.).

In 1890 Congress passed a second Morrill Act to provide a funding mechanism for the existing Land-Grant Institutions created under the Morrill Act of 1862. A significant clause in the 1890 Morrill Act denied funds to any 1862 Land-Grant Institution that discriminated in admission on the basis of "race." Thus, states that had legal separation of the races were allowed to escape the discrimination clause by establishing separate facilities for the colored race. Thus the black 1890 Land-Grant Institutions were born. Currently sixteen of these institutions exist, all having been established by 1909 (table 3.1). Although Tuskegee University, a private institution, was not formally considered an 1890 institution, it is nonetheless currently written into 1890 legislation and is considered one of the 1890 institutions in its purpose and structure. Thus, these institutions are most commonly referred to as the "1890 Institutions (or Black Land-Grant Institutions) and Tuskegee University."

Growth and development of these institutions can be viewed in the terms of the time it took to initiate both four-year and graduate programs and to achieve regional accreditation (table 3.1). As is evident by the late accreditation dates, their development and growth were slow. This chronological lag was primarily the result of different legislation by federal and state governments, where the states denied the Black Land-Grant Institutions funds and support to which they were entitled (Wilson, et al., 1980).

At the outset, these institutions were little more than secondary schools offering the equivalent of a high school education. None of the institutions offered college-level courses until 1916 (Payne, 1970).

Table 3.1
Development History of 1890 Institutions and Tuskegee University

Name Of Institution	Year Founded	Initiated 4-Year Program	Initiated Graduate Program	Regional Accreditation
Alabama A & M University	1875	1939	1958	1963
Alcorn State University	1871	1871	1975	1961
University of Arkansas—Pine Bluff	1873	1929	na	1933
Delaware State College	1891	1947	na	1957
Florida A & M University	1887	1909	1951	1949
Fort Valley State College	1895	1945	1957[a]	1957
Kentucky State University	1886	1929	1972	1939[a]
Langston University	1897	1897[a]	na	1939[a]
Lincoln University	1866	1935	1940	1935
University of Maryland—Eastern Shore	1886	1936	1978	1953
North Carolina A & T State University	1891	1925	1939	1936
Prairie View A & M University	1876	1901	1954	1958[a]
South Carolina State College	1872	1924	1948	1960
Southern University	1880	1922	1957	1958
Tennessee State University	1909	1922	1942	1946
Tuskegee University	1881	1928	1943	1933
Virginia State University	1882	1943	1937	1933

Source: Mayberry, B. D. (ed.). *Development of Research At Historically Black Land-Grant Institutions*. Association of Research Coordinators, 1979.
[a]*Source*: Williams, Thomas T. and Handy Williamson, Jr. "Teaching, and Extension Programs at Predominantly Black Land-Grant Institutions," *Southern Journal of Agricultural Economics*, 17(1985)31-41.

Despite the paucity of funds and other handicaps faced by these institutions, they have made significant contributions to higher education in this country. They have produced over 600,000 graduates, moreover, they currently have an annual enrollment of approximately 60,000 black students and produce over 10,000 graduates per annum. One field of study in these institutions is agricultural economics or agribusiness.

Methodology

The development of agricultural economics programs and degree offerings at 1890 institutions can be traced by investigating factors such as number of institutions offering bachelor and master's degrees in agricultural economics, dates of program inception, enrollment status, growth in number of faculty and level of education, number of tenured faculty, allocation of faculty time to research and teaching, and the general thought or belief concerning current conditions of 1890 universities' agricultural economics programs, and future perceptions of the 1890 administrators and faculty.

The data for this paper were obtained chiefly from a telephone survey administered to various administrators, and chairpersons or faculty members in agricultural economics programs at fifteen of the 1890 institutions. The survey was administered in the fall of 1989 and consisted of a combination of closed and open-ended questions. Given the nature of the data, descriptive statistics are used in presenting the findings.

Findings

The inception dates of a program or degree offering in agricultural economics at some of the 1890 institutions are provided in table 3.2. All of the institutions except one offer a degree or concentration in agricultural economics or agribusiness. A bachelor of science degree in agricultural economics is offered by 10 of the institutions; one in agribusiness is available at 7 of the institutions, with 3 institutions offering a concentration in agribusiness. Currently, only 5 of the 1890 institutions have master's programs: 2 in agricultural economics and 3 in agribusiness (table 3.2).

The first 1890 institution to offer a Bachelor of Science in Agricultural Economics (according to available data) was North Carolina A & T State University in 1951. The latest institution to initiate a degree program (a Master of Science degree in Agricultural Economics), was Tuskegee University December 1988. Only three institutions—Southern University, South Carolina State College, and North Carolina A & T State University—have departments of agricultural economics or agribusiness. The other institutions have programs of study housed under other

schools and in various divisions or departments; they are referred to as
areas, units, or programs.

Table 3.2
Agricultural Economics/Agribusiness Degrees Granted at 1890 Institutions.

1890 Institutions	B.S. Ag. Econ.	B.S. Ag. Bus.	M.S. Ag. Econ.	M.S. Ag. Bus.
Alabama A & M University	X	X	—	X
Alcorn State University	X (1972)[a]	—	—	—
University of Arkansas—Pine Bluff	X (1970s)[a]	X[b]	—	—
Delaware State College	—	X[b]	—	—
Florida A & M University	—	X	—	—
Fort Valley State	X	— (1980)[a]	—	—
Kentucky State University	—	—	—	—
Langston University	X	—	—	—
Lincoln University	X	X[b]	—	—
University of Maryland—Eastern Shore	—	X (1986)[a]	—	—
North Carolina A & T State University	X (1951)[a]	X (1951)[a]	X (1979)[a]	—
Prairie View A & M University	X (1950s)[a]	—	X	—
South Carolina State College	—	X (1983)[a]	—	X (1983)[a]
Southern University	X	X	—	—
Tennessee State University	—	X	—	—
Tuskegee University	—	—	X (1988)[a]	—
Virginia State University	X	—	—	—

[a]Year program was initiated.
[b]Concentration in Agribusiness.

Student enrollment in agricultural economics at these institutions
varies according to the type of degree offered and the location of the
institution. Many of the 1890 institutions located in a predominately

rural area have had the largest enrollment of students (table 3.3). Most of the institutions have indicated that enrollment has been constant or increasing. Some reasons given for the increase have been: the addition of a master's program, higher tuition at other colleges and universities, stringent admission requirements at other institutions, attractiveness of smaller colleges and universities (more personable), distance from competing institutions, recruitment programs, and curriculum changes.

In 1989, based on information received from the survey respondents at 15 of the 1890 institutions, undergraduate students majoring in agriculture accounts for approximately 4.1 percent of the entire student enrollment of 65,500 (table 3.3). Of this 4.1 percent (or 2,712 students), 18 percent (499 students) were enrolled in agricultural economics or agribusiness. The five 1890 institutions offering a master's degree had a combined graduate enrollment of 86 students. Some faculty suggest that enrollment in agricultural economics will continue to spiral upward, especially at places offering a concentration in agribusiness.

Data collected from 14 of the 1890 institutions regarding faculty characteristics yielded a total of 55 agricultural economists at these institutions (table 3.4). Black Americans made up only 40 percent of the agricultural economics faculty located at the 1890 institutions. However, this percentage increased to 75 percent when adding the international faculty (African and Caribbean), which accounted for 35 percent. Moreover, the foreign faculty, black and nonblack, represented over 50 percent of the agricultural economists. The nonblack faculty made up 25 percent of the agricultural economists and the female faculty account for only 5 percent.

In 1979, the total number of agricultural economists at the 14 institutions was 42 (table 3.5). As previously stated, in 1989 that number increased to 55, a 30 percent increase. The faculty number at all the 1890 institutions, except Prairie View A&M University, has either remained constant or increased over the period 1979–1989. At 4 of the institutions, the number of agricultural economists did not change, whereas 9 indicated their number had increased. The largest increase was at South Carolina State College, where the number of agricultural economists increased from 2 to 8.

Special note should be made of this increase and South Carolina State College, since in recent years this school has lost its agriculture programs

Table 3.3
1890 Institutions Enrollment for the University, School of Agriculture, and Agricultural Economics Program, 1989.

1890 Institutions	University	School of Agriculture	Ag. Econ. Programs B.S.	Ag. Econ. Programs M.S.
Alabama A & M University	4,600	375	40	26
Alcorn State University	2,800	130	35	—
University of Arkansas— Pine Bluff	3,800	100	60	—
Delaware State College	2,600	62	—	—
Florida A & M University	6,500	315	50	—
Fort Valley State College	2,000	130	55	—
Kentucky State University	—	—	—	—
Langston University	3,600	20	—	—
Lincoln University	2,800	80	40	—
University of Maryland Eastern Shore	1,500	150	22	—
North Carolina A & T State University	6,200	300	15	45
Prairie View A & M University	5,300	232	50	10
South Carolina State College	4,100	88	77	11
Southern University	8,700	300	30	—
Tennessee State University	7,800	250	25	—
Tuskegee University	3,200	180	—	4
Virginia State College	—	—	—	—
Total	65,500	2,712	499	86

Source: Response from 1890 institutions administrators and faculty.

Table 3.4
Gender and Racial Background of Agricultural Economists
at 1890 Institutions, 1989

	Gender		Race			
			American		International	
1890 Institutions	**Male**	**Female**	**Blk**	**Non Blk**	**Blk**	**Non Blk**
Alabama A & M University	7	0	2	2	0	3
Alcorn State University	3	0	1	0	2	0
University of Arkansas— Pine Bluff	2	1	1	1	1	0
Delaware State University	0	0	0	0	0	0
Florida A & M University	3	0	1	0	2	0
Fort Valley State College	2	1	2	0	1	0
Kentucky State University	0	0	0	0	0	0
Langston University	2	0	1	0	0	1
Lincoln University	2	0	2	0	0	0
University of Maryland— Eastern Shore	3	0	1	0	2	0
North Carolina A & T State University	7	0	4	1	2	0
Prairie View A & M University	2	0	2	0	0	0
South Carolina State College	7	1	2	1	4	1
Southern University	3	1	2	0	2	0
Tennessee State University	5	0	1	0	0	4
Tuskegee University	3	0	0	0	3	0
Virginia State College	0	0	0	0	0	0
Total	51	4	22	5	19	9

Source: Response From 1890 Institutions Administrators and Faculty.

to Clemson. The increase in agricultural economists is the result of a viable agribusiness program initiated in the School of Business.

Only nine of the institutions have agricultural economists who are tenured (table 3.5). Moreover, only 20 or 30 percent of the agricultural economists at all the 1890 institutions have tenure. Over 85 percent of the agricultural economists have their terminal degrees (Ph.D.). The remaining 15 percent have Master of Science degrees.

Since teaching, not research, has been and still is, by design, the primary focus at these institutions, we find that on average, only 37 percent of the faculty time is allotted for research. The other 63 percent is allocated to teaching. Much of the research at these institutions has been in small farm or limited-resource analysis. All the institutions indicated some type of research in this area, perhaps because the 1890 institutions were thrust into research aimed primarily at the small, limited-resource farm sector primarily due to three factors: (1) 1862 institutions had little or no interest in this area of research, (2) the federal government allotted funds to 1890 universities for research in this area, and (3) most of the 1890 institutions were located in limited-resource communities and had a history of serving the needs of the economically disadvantaged.

The information in table 3.5 seems to indicate that the foundation for developing strong degree programs (B.S. and M.S.) has been set. Although the development process has been slow and constrained, tenacity is paying off. Most of the 1890 institutions have indicated that their major problem was not enrollment, but funding and manpower. Many cannot attract faculty due to the lack of sufficient federal and state funds. Without these funds, 1890 institutions have had difficulty offering tenured positions. Thus, many 1890 institutions have depended on faculty's willingness to commit to giving a part of themselves to an institution devoted to serving the economically and socially disadvantaged.

In light of the above, all the institutions have indicated that there is a future for agricultural economics at the 1890 institutions. However, a major problem has occurred when they compete with or duplicate programs of the 1862 institutions. As the 1890 institutions continue to upgrade their curriculum, upgrade their facilities, change people's perception of their institutions and programs of study, offer additional programs (for example a master's degree), cater to more than just

Table 3.5
Faculty Number, Tenure, Level of Education of Agricultural Economists at
1890 Institutions, 1989.

Institution	Number of Faculty 1979[a]	1989	Number of Tenured Faculty	Highest Degree Ph.D.	M.S.	Faculty Appointment Mean Percent Research	Teaching
Alabama A & M University	1	7	7	5	2	25%	75%
Alcorn State University	1	3	0	2	1	33%	64%
University of Arkansas— Pine Bluff	2	3	0	2	1	56%	46%
Delaware State College							
Florida A & M University	0	3	0	2	1	25%	75%
Fort Valley State College	3	3	2	3	0	53%	47%
Kentucky State University							
Langston University	2	2	0	1	1	0	100%
Lincoln University	1	2	0	2	0	25%	75%
University of Maryland— Eastern Shore	1	3	0	3	0	50%	50%
North Carolina A & T State University	7	7	1	7	0	65%	35%
Prairie View A & M University	3	2	2	2	0	25%	75%
South Carolina State University	2	8	3	7	1	25%	75%
Southern University	3	4	3	4	0	50%	50%
Tennessee State University	3	5	1	4	1	65%	35%
Tuskegee University	1	3	1	3	0	30%	70%
Virginia State College							

[a]*Source*: Edward Wilson, et al., *Strengthening 1890 Land-Grant Institutions* (1980). All other information obtained through telephone survey of 1890 institutions administrators and faculty.

minorities, and get the administrators interested in their programs—agricultural economics at the 1890 institutions will remain a vital discipline of study in these institution's schools of agriculture, economics, or business.

The Case of North Carolina A & T State University

Since neither time nor space will allow us to provide an evolutionary account of the development of agricultural economics programs at each of the 1890 institutions, we will focus our attention on North Carolina A & T State University. The survey indicated that North Carolina A & T State University was the first 1890 institution to develop both an undergraduate and graduate program in agricultural economics, and a brief synopsis of its evolution may be helpful since many of the other 1890 institutions may have developed in a similar manner. (The primary sources for this synopsis are various issues of North Carolina A & T Bulletin; Self-Study Reports, 1969 and 1970).

North Carolina A & T State University was established as the "A and M College for the Colored Race" by an act of the General Assembly of North Carolina, ratified March 9, 1891. The college began operation in Raleigh during the school year of 1890–1891, before the passage of the state law creating it. A plan was worked out with Shaw University in Raleigh where the college had operated as an annex to Shaw University during the years 1890–1893.

The law of 1891 stipulated that the college should be permanently located in whichever city or town would offer a suitable inducement. A group of interested citizens in Greensboro donated fourteen acres of land for a site and $11,000 to aid in constructing buildings. This amount was supplemented by an appropriation of $2,500 from the General Assembly. The first building was completed in 1893 and the college opened in Greensboro during the fall of that year. In 1915, the name of the institution was changed to the Agricultural and Technical College of North Carolina for the Colored Race by an act of the state legislature.

The scope of the college program has been enlarged to take care of new demands. The General Assembly authorized the institution to grant the Master of Science degree in education and certain other fields in 1939, and the first master's degree was awarded in 1941. The School of Nursing was established by an act of the state legislature in 1953, and its first class was graduated in 1957.

In 1957, the General Assembly repealed previous acts describing the purpose of the college, and redefined its mission as follows:

> The primary purpose of the College should be to teach the Agricultural and Technical Arts and Sciences and such branches of learning as related thereto; the training of teachers, supervisors, and administrators for the public schools of the State, including the preparation of such teachers, supervisors, and administrators for the Master's degree. Such other programs of a professional or occupational nature may be offered as shall be approved by the North Carolina board of Higher Education, consistent with the appropriations made therefore. (North Carolina A & T State University, 1970)

On October 30, 1971, the General Assembly ratified an act to consolidate the institutions of higher learning in North Carolina. Under the provisions of this act, North Carolina Agricultural and Technical State University became a constituent institution of the University of North Carolina effective July 1, 1972.

Departmental History

A review of the bulletins of North Carolina A & T, beginning in 1924, allow us to chart the genesis of the Department of Agricultural Economics and Rural Sociology at North Carolina A & T State University. In the academic year 1924–1925, two courses, Economics II (Farm Management) and Economics III (Marketing), were required courses for a B.S. degree in Agriculture. The course description for Economics II read:

> A study of farming as a business; types of farming, farm layouts, labor problems, farm tenure and leases, farm credits, the choice of a farm; starting in the business of farming etc. (Bulletin:42)

The Economics III course description read:

> A study of the world's sources of food and raw materials and the conditions under which each is produced and consumed. The marketing and great markets for the products of both the plant and animal industries. The function of the middlemen and institutions, transportation, storage, speculation, weakness of present system, cooperative marketing among farmers. (Ibid.)

These course descriptions provide historical foundation for many courses currently taught in agricultural economics classes. During the academic year 1926–1927, Economics II and III were renamed Agricultural Economics IV and II, respectively. Also, two other courses joined the name change: Farm Accounting (Agricultural Economics III), and Economics Principles (Agricultural Economics I). Again, these were required courses for a B.S. degree in the School of Agriculture— Agricultural Economics before Economics is not uncommon in Land-Grant Institutions.

During the academic year 1930–1931, the Agricultural Economics courses were transferred from the School of Agriculture to the School of Education and General Studies. However, they were still required courses for students majoring in agriculture. Again, there were name changes in the courses.

Although a B.S. degree in agricultural economics was not offered until 1951, the 1940–1941 Bulletin mentions a Department of Agricultural Economics and Rural Sociology under the Graduate School. Thus, a graduate degree in agricultural economics was one of the first degrees offered by the Graduate School. Moreover, the agricultural economics courses were listed in The Graduate School under the heading Department of Agricultural Economics and Rural Sociology from the academic years 1940–1941 to 1960–1961.

Beginning the academic year 1951–1952, the bulletin listed the department in the School of Agriculture, offering a B.S. degree in Agricultural Economics. The first chair of the Department was the late Dr. Frederick A. Williams, followed by Dr. Vernon A. Johnson. The department is managed by a chairman, with close faculty involvement. There are standing committees on curricula, recruitment, and admissions (to the graduate program).

References

Bulletin of North Carolina Agricultural and Technical State University. Various issues 1924–1989.

The International Encyclopedia of Higher Education. Asa S. Knowles (Ed.). Volume 2A. San Francisco: Jossey-Bass Publisher, 1977, p. 209–211.

Mayberry, B.D., ed. *Development of Research at Historically Black Land-Grant Institutions*. Tuskegee, Ala.: The Bicentennial Committee of the Association of Research Directors, 1976.

North Carolina A & T State University, Department of Economics. "Self-Study Report." Greensboro, N.C.: North Carolina A & T State University, 1969.

——. School of Agriculture. "Self-Study Report." Greensboro, N.C.: North Carolina A & T State University, 1970.

Payne, Bill. "Forgotten . . . But Not Gone: The Negro Land-Grant Colleges." *Civil Rights Digests*, vol. 3, no. 2, Government Printing Office, Spring 1970.

Schuh, G. Edward. "Revitalizing Land-Grant Universities: It's Time to Regain Relevance." *Choice*, The American Agricultural Economics Association, Second Quarter 1986, pp. 6–10.

Taylor, Henry C. *The Story of Agricultural Economics in the United States, 1840–1932.* Ames, Iowa: Iowa State College Press, 1952.

Williams, Thomas T. and Handy Williamson, Jr. "Teaching, Research, and Extension Programs at Predominantly Black Land-Grant Institutions." *Southern Journal of Agricultural Economics* 17 (1985), pp. 31–41.

Wilson, Edward, et al. *Strengthening 1890 Land-Grant Institutions.* Report to the U.S. Department of Agriculture, Lincoln University, Jefferson City, Mo., 1980.

PART II

A Contemporary View of 1890 Institutions

Tuskegee University, Tuskegee, Alabama. Susanne Loomis, Photographer.

4

Resident Instruction Programs at 1890 Institutions

Leroy Davis

Resident instruction has been the principal focus of many 1890 institutions until 1969 when these institutions also began to receive funds for research and extension programs under the now Evans Allen funds. Resident instruction has received state funding as a component of the agricultural and mechanical institution. Thus, resident instruction has been a state function and has failed to garner federal funds as the other two principal functions of land-grant institutions.

Changes in funding and other areas have caused a decline in the number of students and the number of resident instruction programs at 1890 institutions. Some of the effects of this decline have been a general reduction in the rural population, a decrease in the number of farms, especially the number of small farms in the South where most of the 1890 institutions are located.

The move toward efficiency and accountability in higher educational programs has led to a reduction in the number of 1890 institutions with resident instruction programs; even fewer have degree programs in agricultural economics. However, much of the increase in demand for agricultural graduates in agricultural economics has been over the last two decades. Of the seventeen 1890 institutions, only half have two or more agricultural economists on their staffs, thus giving rise to heavy teaching loads and little opportunity for research and extension activities.

Changing Student Composition

One of the more significant transitions at 1890 universities is the changing student mix. Fewer and fewer students each year have farm experience and fewer reside in rural areas. There is more of an urban/suburban mix which has occurred in the past fifteen years. More female students are now matriculating at 1890 universities in the colleges of agriculture. Agricultural economics and agribusiness are more often the majors of choice. There has also been an influx of international students. This growth in international students occurred in the late 1970s and early 1980s. However, the number of international students has leveled off and the absolute number has actually declined during the past five years because of the changes in world trade relationships and the debt crisis confronting middle- and low-income nations. Despite reduced numbers, improvement has been observed in the quality of those entering the agricultural economics and agribusiness programs. This improvement in the students can be attributed in part to the increased availability of scholarships. More scholarships are still essential to attracting better quality students.

Employment Opportunities

Traditionally the graduates of the colleges of agriculture and agricultural economics programs at 1890 universities found employment principally as vocational agriculture teachers at both predominantly black and all-black high schools in the South. Some found job opportunities as county extension agents. In the 1960s and 1970s, the U.S. Department of Agriculture (USDA) agencies made some special effort to employ student trainees and then made available permanent jobs. At first, employment was outside the South in western, midwestern and border states. Later employment became available in southern states.

In the late 1970s and the 1980s agribusiness firms began to seek and employ high-quality graduates. Some summer internships were developed along with co-op programs in various areas. Most of the jobs were in the area of sales and marketing. More recently positions in management have become available, and the trend toward agribusiness employment is likely to continue for some time in the future. Salary levels, fringe benefits and good working conditions are responsible for this trend.

One area that is relatively untapped is the foreign service, due to the lack of international experience and interest of most of our students. It is expected, with some degree of real world observation, that the foreign service will be a good opportunity for graduates of 1890 universities.

Curriculum Changes

For many years the curriculum in agricultural economics at 1890 universities remained unchanged from what it was immediately follow-ing World War II. The curriculum was designed to train vocational agriculture teachers and extension workers. This orientation accounted in part for the stagnation in the curriculum. During recent years there has been a movement toward the development of "required" options. Such options include marketing, agribusiness, management, and busi-ness. These options were designed to meet the demand for employment in agribusiness industries and governmental agencies.

Also, a trend toward offering international development courses into the curriculum has been established. This trend has been caused by efforts of the Agency for International Development (AID) to bring minorities in as employees. AID made efforts to offer grants and contracts to 1890 universities in the early 1970s. However, few 1890 universities have received large contracts to perform development assis-tance work. AID has mostly offered small grants and limited contracts.

Some other curriculum changes include more computer science cour-ses, systems analysis, mathematics and statistics. The quality and flexibility in the curriculum have both improved over the past decade. This trend is likely to continue as the competition for students increases.

The Role of 1890 Institutions

The 1890 institutions have well-defined and important roles to play in resident instruction. One of the continuing roles is to educate the poor and disadvantaged citizens in the southern region, the nation, and the world. These institutions provide educational services to first-genera-tion college students. Some expertise and experience have been developed to meet the needs of this group of people. Another important role is that of serving as feeder programs to graduate schools at 1862 institutions. Most of the black American students who attend graduate school in colleges of agriculture at 1862 institutions obtain their first degrees at 1890 institutions. There is no immediate prospect that this trend will change over the next decade.

However, 1890 universities must develop graduate programs to augment their research components. There will be a void in the total composition of the land-grant functions of 1890 universities without their having graduate students to help with the research activities.

Demand for Agricultural Economists

In the past two decades, the demand for graduates of 1890 universities has increased. This has been caused to some degree by the increase in research and extension funding levels by the federal government via USDA. However, the demand has leveled off because real funding allocation has actually declined over the past few years. Some of the decline in the demand has been caused by the decline in Affirmative Action programs at 1862 institutions and other institutions in this country.

Some demand increase was caused in the 1970s and 1980s by the retirement of older professors, many of whom had been hired immediately following World War II. However, future demand is likely to come from non-educational institutions in the next decade.

Critical Issues

Several critical issues still face 1890 institutions in the coming decade and into the twenty-first century. (1) Will agricultural economics programs be able to survive under increasing pressure of accountability and efficiency? (2) Can these programs continue to exist as undergraduate departments only? (3) Under present salary and working conditions, will 1890 institutions be able to continue to attract high-quality and dedicated faculty members? (4) Are there viable opportunities for combining agricultural economics programs with economics and business programs? (5) Are there opportunities for cooperative programs with 1862 institutions? (6) Can good teaching garner respect in a research- and publication-oriented discipline? (7) Is the role of training the impoverished and the less-well-prepared important in a technocratic, post-agrarian, post-industrial society? (8) Does the market force legislate against the small departments and 1890 universities? How the 1890 institutions handle these issues will determine the ability to continue their proud traditions.

References

Cooperative State Research Service, U.S. Department of Agriculture. *1988–89 Salary Analysis. For State Agricultural Experiment Stations, Forestry Schools, Colleges of 1890 and Tuskegee University, and Schools Veterinary Medicine.* Washington, D.C.: U.S. Department of Agriculture, 1989.

Jones, Barbara, A. P. "NEA Presidential Address: Economics Programs at Historically Black Colleges and Universities." *The Review of Black Political Economy*, vol. 16, no. 3 (1988), pp. 5–14.

Mayberry, B.D., ed. *Development of Research at Historically Black Land-Grant Institutions.* Tuskegee, Ala.: The Bicentennial Committee of the Association of Research Directors, 1976.

National Research Council. *Educating the Next Generation of Agricultural Scientist.* Washington, D.C.: National Academy Press, 1988.

5

Status of Agricultural Research Programs at 1890 Land-Grant Institutions and Tuskegee University

McKinley Mayes

The Morrill Acts of 1862 and 1890, the Hatch Act of 1887, and the Smith Lever Act of 1914 constitute the legislative foundation of today's land-grant colleges' teaching, research, and extension services. Indeed, those three functions represent the essence of the land-grant college—teaching, research, and extension services. To be succinct, the land-grant college was created to foster and to personify a certain philosophy—that philosophy is best reflected in the statement made by William Oxley Thompson in 1912. "The land-grant college is to be an institution that is opened for the good it can do; for the people it can serve, for the science it can promote, and for the civilization it can advance."

In 1862, at the time of the first Morrill Act, 90 percent of America's Black population was in slavery. The land-grant colleges that developed were essentially all Caucasian in composition, and even after the Civil War, Black Americans were barred from admission both by law and custom. When the second Morrill Act was passed in 1890, primarily to obtain more operating money for the colleges, Congress added a "separate-but-equal" provision authorizing the establishment of colleges for Blacks. Seventeen southern and border states took advantage of the Act, creating institutions that are referred to as colleges of 1890.

Today, these seventeen institutions and Tuskegee University continue to produce agricultural experts and other professionals who are successfully employed by agribusiness corporations, U.S. Department of Agricultrue (USDA), and other governmental agencies.

Cooperative State Research Service (CSRS)

USDA Role in Funding Research at 1890 Universities

CSRS administers the state Experiment Station, Schools of Forestry, the 1890 colleges and Tuskegee University, and special and competitive grant funds provided through USDA to states to supplement and support local research and education resident instruction. CSRS scientific staff reviews proposed research and research progress. They help plan and coordinate research; and they encourage establishing and maintaining cooperation by and between states, and between states and federal agencies.

A small level of financial support began in 1967: $283,000, an average of $16,600 per institution. A significant level began in fiscal year (FY) 1972: $8,830,000, an average of $522,529. The FY 1978 level was $14,153,000, an average of $832,529, and in FY 1979 it was $16,260,000, an average of $962,353. Fourteen institutions receive more than $1 million each year. These are: Fort Valley State College, Kentucky State University, Lincoln University, Alcorn State University, North Carolina A & T State University, Tennessee State University, Prairie View A & M University, Tuskegee University, Alabama A & M University, University of Arkansas—Pine Bluff, Southern University, Langston University, South Carolina State University and Virginia State University. FY 1989 funding was $24,333,000 with an average of $1,431,353 for each institution.

Planning and Coordination

The 1890 institutions are an integral part of America's highly successful agricultural research system. This nationwide research effort has helped to develop the most productive and efficient agricultural enterprise in the world. Researchers at 1890 institutions have made important contributions to this effort. Other vital components of the system include the Agricultural Experiment Stations at the 1862 land-grant institutions, other public and private universities, and state and federal government agencies, especially those in USDA. The success and efficiency of the nation's agricultural research program is facilitated by a highly effective planning, coordinating, and funding system. The heart of this system is a partnership, administering federal formula funds and coordinating research planning and budgeting for the land-grant institution.

With the beginning of sustained federal funds for 1890 agricultural research in 1967, these institutions became a part of this highly coordinated system. This participation was strengthened by the 1977 Evans-Allen legislation, which requires that each 1890 institution work with its corresponding 1862 land-grant university to develop jointly an annual plan of work which is submitted to CSRS for approval. This process ensures that unnecessary duplication of effort is avoided and complementary research programs are encouraged.

Current 1890 Research Emphasis

The 1890 institutions have developed a multitude of research programs to respond to the variety of problems and opportunities in their respective states. In just a few short years—less than two decades—scientists at these colleges and universities have made significant contributions in animal science, crop science, natural resources, human health and nutrition, and rural development. In addition to advancing basic scientific knowledge and providing scientific training in these areas, the results of 1890 agricultural research have benefitted all kinds of people in all economic and social circumstances.

Many 1890 institutions are working on ways to increase the productivity and profitability of animal production systems. Some researchers are concentrating on minor livestock species, such as goats, rabbits, and earthworms, which are particularly well suited for small farm operations.

Researchers at 1890 institutions have partially established the nutritional requirements of dairy goats and have identified a milk replacer for kids. Such results enable these institutions to provide ongoing technical and managerial assistance to goat producers.

More traditional livestock species and production systems also receive attention at 1890 institutions. For example, scientists have evaluated feeding systems for beef cattle to lower production costs, studied methods to improve reproductive efficiency in sheep and pigs, and established ways to increase productivity in poultry and egg operations.

Sweet potatoes are planted on 100,000 acres in the United States and are a $110 million-a-year business. However, high production costs are forcing growers' net income to decline. Teams of scientists at several 1890 institutions are working on various aspects of this problem.

Scientists at 1890 institutions have developed improved production methods for such horticultural crops as muskmelons, tomatoes, and green beans.

An adequate diet and good health are the foundation for a productive life. Scientists at 1890 institutions long have been concerned about the nutrition and health of citizens in their states, especially economically disadvantaged populations. Much research has been conducted in this area, including evaluations of nutrient-assessment methods, investigations of food safety, and studies of the nutritional status of adolescents, senior citizens, and low-income families.

These examples illustrate the sophistication and scope of agricultural research at the 1890 institutions. In a short time, and with limited resources, these institutions have developed significant and respected research programs.

Research is never completed, however, until the results are shared with other scientists and laypersons. This philosophy is one of the pillars of the land-grant system. Like their sister 1862 institutions, the 1890 institutions have a long tradition of direct service to the people of their states.

Priorities for Future Research

The research priorities established by the 1890 institutions reflect both their overall mission and their historical commitment. They are designed to advance scientific knowledge, as well as to serve the constituents of these institutions.

Farming Systems

Alternative production systems that take into account various agricultural practices and policies, as well as social and economic factors, need to be devised to increase the profitability of farming operations.

Livestock Production

Minor livestock species are particularly suitable for small farmers because they require low capital investment. Additional research is needed to determine the most desirable and profitable means of utilizing feed grains, pastures, forages, and other crop by-products for the production of these species.

Biotechnology

Biotechnology is receiving a great deal of attention throughout the agricultural community and promises to revolutionize the agricultural industry.

Crop Production and Marketing

New techniques for plant breeding and improved cultural practices must be developed to cut production costs and increase yields of existing agricultural crops.

Aquaculture

The production of selected fish species holds potential for converting feed concentrates into animal protein more efficiently than other known animal systems, thus contributing to global animal protein needs.

Family and Community Development

Decisions related to family and community development are increasing in importance and complexity and require more information than ever before.

Human Nutrition and Health

More information is needed on the nutritional requirements of the elderly, adolescents, pregnant women, and minorities.

Water and Soil Management and Conservation

Water is becoming an increasingly scarce resource, making it necessary to determine the optimum combination of water and other inputs for maximum yield and economic returns.

Development of Scientific and Professional Expertise

The development of scientific and professional expertise for a well-developed, high-tech agriculture industry is critical. The need for qualified scientists, especially from the minority community, to fill professional positions is very serious and is expected to intensify in the near future.

6

Extension Programs at the 1890 Land-Grant Institutions

Dan Godfrey and Alton Franklin

This current assessment of Extension Programs at the 1890 Land-Grant Institutions and Tuskegee University comes primarily from a recent U.S. Department of Agriculture (USDA) publication, *Serving People In Need*, probably the most recent up-to-date account of current programming in the 1890 institutions. First, it consists of a brief historical perspective of the development of 1890 Land-Grant Institutions with emphasis on Extension Programs. Then, it focuses on some emerging issues facing extension in general, and 1890 institutions in particular, given our program target audience of small-scale farmers, communities, and youth, as well as older Americans.

In 1890, Congress passed legislation now known as the Second Morrill Act. The First Morrill Act, passed in 1862, established a means for federal contributions to the support of a college or university in each of the states. The Second Morrill Act extended the benefits of the Land-Grant Institutions to the black population of sixteen states. It did so by designating a traditionally black institution in each of these states as a Land-Grant Institution. The Second Morrill Act of 1890 also designated Tuskegee University (then Tuskegee Institute) as one of these seventeen institutions. Today, these seventeen institutions are commonly referred to as the Historically Black Land-Grant Institutions, "the 1890s".

Although the Smith-Lever Act of 1914 formally established the Cooperative Extension System, this legislation was in some regards only a positive response to what was already being done. Many of those who are recognized as the founding pioneers of Cooperative Extension had already set the groundwork by the time the Smith-Lever Act was passed, and some of the most important of these pioneers—Booker T. Washington, for example—were affiliated with our group of 1890 institutions and Tuskegee University.

Nearly twenty-five years later, the Smith-Lever Act established the Cooperative Extension Service as a joint effort of the USDA and the Land-Grant Institutions in each state. It also provided for county-level participation. Additionally, the act directed our 1890 schools to work in cooperation with our 1862 counterparts to extend the benefits of the Cooperative Extension System to the black population of our respective states. This arrangement has lasted for seventy-five years. In the mid-1960s, Congress responded to the need to reestablish the 1890 Extension Programs with legislation providing earmarked funding to be administered by each state's Cooperative Extension Service.

Extension Programs at 1890 schools now function within guidelines established by the Food and Agriculture Act of 1977. Chief among the differences between the 1977 and the 1972 legislation which it replaced is the elimination of the role of the state Extension Service in distributing funds to the 1890 Extension Programs in most of the states with two Land-Grant schools. This act—and subsequent legislation enacted— provide for the autonomy of the 1890 Extension Programs in allocating the funds that were set aside by Congress.

Our Target Audience

The 1890 Extension Programs have targeted people with limited economic resources who have often lacked the educational background of most Americans. They are the people who have needed help the most. But the same disadvantages that have placed them in need have caused them to build walls around themselves. The custom-tailored 1890 Extension Programs have addressed their individual needs.

What are these needs? And, why are they the concern of all Americans? Consider the following:

- During the past 30 years, the percentage of Americans living on farms has dropped from 10 percent to 2.4 percent of the overall population.

- Most studies agree that the United States now has the highest rate of teenage pregnancy of any industrialized nation. Families headed by teenage mothers often receive public welfare. Nationally, more than half of all welfare expenditures are for households in which the mother was a teenager when her first child was born. Researchers estimate the annual public cost for such households at more than $15 billion.

- The number of people age sixty-five and older who live alone will rise from nearly a million to around 13.3 million by the year 2020. Among the elderly living alone, poverty has been highest among minority groups. These figures break down as follows, 43 percent for Hispanics, compared with 16 percent for whites.

To reach the hard-to-reach, our Extension Programs have responded with innovation in both organizational structure as well as programming. One proven example has been the use by many 1890 Extension Programs of paraprofessionals. These paraprofessionals, usually community members themselves, have often worked one-on-one with families and individuals to open channels of communication between those in need and Extension staffers throughout the land-grant system. Our Extension Programs also meet the unique needs of clientele with information and educational programs that are innovative, even those programs that are still on the drawing board, but malleable once implemented. We should all keep in mind that programs to serve people are best when they are planned and designed for the people they serve.

Now let me turn our attention to particular audience categories.

Small-Scale Farmers: Alternative Agriculture Can Make the Difference

The plight of the small-scale farmer has always been the focus of much of our 1890 Extension activity, especially as economic adversity has hit more and more of these farmers during this decade. Our Extension Programs have met this need by increasing our educational efforts, targeted to small-scale farmers. Approximately 20,000 farmers are served by the 1890 Extension Programs and these small-scale farmers are our clients. We are working hard to equip these farmers with the competitive edge essential to survival.

The publication *Serving People In Need* provides some specific examples of pragmatic efforts by 1890 schools directed to small farmers.

In a joint effort that has involved a private philanthropic organization and a federal agency, one state Extension Program has been involved in an ambitious effort to improve the genetic quality (and eventually the profitability) of livestock owned by small farmers in a twelve-county region. But good breeding stock is expensive, and with each generation of low returns from the sale of the animals, these new breeds have been becoming more unaffordable. So, 1890 Extension specialists have solved this problem by obtaining a grant and using it to purchase genetically strong animals—beef cattle, dairy goats, rabbits, and swine. These animals have been loaned out to producers who needed them most. However, this loan has not been without an interest charge. Farmers have been required to return not only the animal they borrowed, but also an offspring. Both animals have then been made available to other qualified farmers. It is easy to understand how the process has become known as "passing the gift."

A similar project coordinated by another 1890 Extension Program focused on beef cattle. In addition to improving the quality of cattle with better breeding stock, this effort also entailed improving the farmer's knowledge and practices of feeds, pasture management, and other aspects of livestock production. Results included a 20 percent increase in the size of calves, a 15 percent increase in the number of calves weaned, and a 35 percent increase in the number of calves marketed.

In another state, the 1890 Extension Program effort assisted small-scale farmers in becoming more competitive by providing financial counseling. For some farmers, learning how to keep accurate records, so they can determine where they are making money and where they are losing it, is the difference between success and failure. For others, information on how to borrow wisely and restructure debt is a key ingredient.

In addition, several 1890 Extension Programs have assisted small-scale farmers in setting up farmers' markets, which give them a competitive edge by "cutting out the middle man."

In another state, the 1890 Extension Program has carried the farmers' market concept a step further—to a farmers' cooperative. Through cooperation with another federal agency, farmers have begun by cultivating fruits and vegetables they have never grown before.

Now, another 1890 Extension Program is working to introduce two new crops—hot peppers and green peanuts—in areas of the state where small-scale farmers can no longer make a living on row crops.

To add to these examples, one new joint project, funded by the W. K. Kellogg Foundation, involving North Carolina A & T and Fort Valley State in Georgia, makes use of video tapes to convey new practices involved in producing alternative enterprises to small-scale farmers. Specifically, North Carolina A & T and Fort Valley State College are jointly developing a series of eight video tapes, entitled "Ways To Grow." Such enterprises as rabbit production, fowls, catfish, shiitake mushrooms, small woodlots, ornamentals, etc., are among tapes already developed. These tapes are now being distributed with a minimum recovery cost for the blank tape and reproduction.

Communities: We Need Them, They Need Revitalization

Often communities cannot respond to the needs of their citizens because the communities themselves are in need. Too often they are out of step with the times; they have been left behind, according to *Serving People in Need*. Revitalizing these communities so that they, in turn, will be able to respond to the needs of individuals is another undertaking of our 1890 Extension Programs. Specifically, our 1890 Extension Program has faced up to the problem of out-migration, and the result is a special-needs USDA project called the "Landownership Information Project." It began with research to determine who was leaving and why, and the research quickly pointed to a key factor: black farmers in the South are losing their farmland at two and one-half times the rate of white farmers (U.S. Commission on Civil Rights Report, 1982). It was clear that our commitment to agriculture was already in place: we had a successful Farm Opportunities Program that was supplying farmers with technological assistance. So, the focus of the Landownership Information Project became education. The cooperation of other agencies was secured, and thus the primary objective became educating farmers.

When needs of rural communities have been unique, the response of 1890 Extension has been tailored to those needs. In one instance, 1890 Extension assisted a community in obtaining a one-half million dollar grant to improve its water system. In another state, 1890 Extension staff assisted two isolated communities in obtaining their first telephone service.

Although 1890 Extension Programs have worked extensively to revitalize communities in rural areas, much has been done to revitalize urban communities—particularly communities in depressed, inner-city areas. For example, in an inner-city area, an 1890 home economist conducts classes in the waiting room of a medical clinic. To better meet the needs of all concerned, she has learned to tap into available community resources not previously accessed by extension staff.

The first task in strengthening and stabilizing families is to locate families in need among the hard-to-reach clientele served by the 1890 Extension Programs. The next task is to decide what to do to meet their needs. The real obstacle to education has been the clientele's lack of reading skills. The 1890 Extension staff has solved this problem of limited reading ability with a series of workshops with more graphics than printed materials.

The 1890 Extension specialist looked first at the skills and materials available to clientele and then tailored an educational effort to fit both needs and resources. In many cases, assessing clientele resources has uncovered an undeveloped information resource. This was the case of a joint effort in three states. Often in many rural communities of the South, when trouble strikes families turn to the local minister for help in coping with life's stresses and problems.

Several 1890 Extension efforts approach the goal of strengthening families from a different angle—they function to keep existing families strong. One such program is "Education for Parenting." More than 21,000 teenagers have been reached through this educational series designed to give youth cause to think seriously before beginning a family. The curriculum includes a three-year, home-study course and a bimonthly newsletter series. The result of the effort is a decline in the rate of teenage pregnancy in twelve of the thirteen counties in the target area. In one county, the incidence of teenage pregnancy was reduced by 12 percent.

Also in our own state, 1890 Extension staffers work in conjunction with the 1862 Cooperative Extension staff to strengthen at-risk families through a program called "Partners-In-Learning." In many of today's families, problems first occur when children are young. "Partners-In-Learning" brings parents and children aged six to eight into a 4-H learning environment, paving the way for involvement in 4-H when the children are older. Currently, 10 percent of all 4-H participants in the state are former "Partners-In-Learning" participants, and we have indication of its great success.

Youth: Offering Alternatives

Many children today are not getting the support and attention at home that children of previous generations received. Among the clientele served by the 1890 Extension Programs are youth of the inner-city. Often, the 1890 Extension Programs have become models as the inner-city youth's problems become problems for other population segments as well. People who need advice seek out experience, and the experience that 1890 Extension workers have gained in their dealing with disadvantaged youth is sought out.

Also, studies support the contention that across the United States, college enrollment in agriculture and related fields has been steadily declining for several years, a trend many find alarming. To combat this problem, our 1890 Extension Programs are responding with efforts to motivate youth toward agricultural study and careers. Specifically, minorities and economically disadvantaged youths are visiting our 1890 Land-Grant Institutions to learn more about career in agriculture and related fields. Most of these programs are conducted during the summer. Some last for days; others for as long as two weeks. Their common goal is to show youth that there is much more opportunity in agriculture than "just farming."

What about Efforts Focused on Older Americans: Assets That Must Not Become Liabilities

Isolation is crippling the lives of millions of Americans in certain segments of society, and one of those segments is the elderly. To target the needs of this specialized clientele, our Extension Program noted that

"People who are approaching retirement need information on role transition and elderly assistance." Another objective was to "acquaint the elderly with knowledge and skills that will prepare them in facing dilemmas." To meet these objectives, teams of Extension specialists, community leaders, paraprofessionals, and home economists have been assembled. These teams have provided information through workshops, group meetings, home visits, and at blood pressure monitoring centers that have been established as part of the effort.

Taking up where this program leaves off was another 1890 Extension effort implemented at a state hospital for the chronically ill: "The project was planned to meet the needs of many patients who missed their life in a rural setting. Many patients had been avid gardeners in younger years, and they cherished the idea of being able to dig down into the earth again."

Our 1890 Extension Programs have targeted areas with a number of retirees who had worked as professionals prior to retirement. The 1890 institutions have implemented programs to enlist retirees as volunteers and to utilize their contributions to extend and support Extension work. It has worked. Teachers, ministers, a public health nurse, a computer programmer, and a retired Extension agent have been among those enlisted in these pilot efforts. Unlike many other volunteers—capable and willing, but in need of supervision and direction—these retirees could be handed a project, such as a blood pressure screening clinic, and left to it while Extension personnel turned energies to other matters.

Emerging Issues: Our New Challenge

As the Cooperative Extension System prepares for the twenty-first century, the emphasis is on *strategic planning* and *issues programming*. The focus is now on methodology—molding programs to fit the critical national issues that need to be addressed by Extension's nationwide educational network.

Issues programming is not new to the 1890 Extension Programs. These programs have a tradition of looking first at the needs of people and next at available resources in order to best utilize them to get the job done. Throughout their history, budget and staff limitations have dictated that the 1890 institutions mold their programs to current issues and concerns of clients.

The 1890 Extension Programs will continue to consider carefully those *issues* they *target*, and give priority to addressing those issues where results will be most significant. And, they will continue to address issues in the context of the *overall mission* and *values* of the Cooperative Extension System. Our 1890 programs must have support for the issues they choose to address from the Cooperative Extension System and the general public. Successful programming addresses one issue and paves the way for others to be addressed at the same time.

To complete the transition from disciplinary programming to issues programming, our 1890 Extension Programs must *reevaluate staffing* strategies with the emphasis on interdisciplinary teamwork. Also, the need for more specialized skills among our county-level personnel is increasing: 1890 programs must gear future staff training and support to meet this need. Another growing demand is for applied research at county as well as state levels.

As we plan for the future, our 1890 Extension Programs will cope with continuing changes in resources as a result of other service agencies programming to meet issues. Resources themselves will also be different. Previously, our Extension Programs have turned almost exclusively to the land-grant universities for resources. When programs are developed from an issues perspective, knowledge and expertise from outside the land-grant system will also be needed.

Future funding for programs is another concern. Presently, our 1890 Extension Programs are funded almost entirely by the U.S. Congress through the USDA Extension Service.

Our 1890 Extension Programs must respond to the close tie between issues programming and public concerns with a restructured accountability and evaluation system. To the same publics whose concerns are addressed, our programs need accessible information on efforts to address these concerns.

At the same time, as we emphasize methodology and issues programming as the way of the future, our 1890 Extension Programs cannot neglect other pressing issues despite their topical nature. All indications are that America is rapidly moving toward a service industry economy. What implications does this hold for limited-resource and other 1890 Extension Program clientele? How can the 1890 programs better reconcile the high technology needs of commercial farmers with those of small-scale farmers?

The current challenge for our 1890 Extension Programs is formidable. We must attend to the present and future with equal diligence. Our 1890 Extension Programs have met formidable challenges before and that record speaks for itself. Our programming over the last several decades has made a difference in the lives of many Americans. The challenge is for it to do so in the future.

References

U.S. Commission on Civil Rights. *The Decline of Black Farming in America.* Washington, D.C.: U.S. Government Printing Office, February, 1982.

U.S. Department of Agriculture. *Serving People in Need.* Extension Service, Program Aid Number 1418. Washington, D.C.: U.S. Department of Agriculture, 1988.

7

International Involvement of Historically Black Land-Grant Institutions in AID-Supported Development Activities and Programs

Handy Williamson, Jr. and Collin C. Weir

The intent of this chapter is to provide a description of the 1890 land-grant universities' involvement in international development activities, undertaken cooperatively with the Agency for International Development (AID). It should be noted that while this paper covers activities undertaken during the recent decade (1979–1989), most of the universities have had significant involvement of much longer durations. For example, Tuskegee University's international development activities date back more than thirty-five years. Tuskegee University has had successful engagements in institution building, research, and technical assistance projects in the countries of Liberia, Upper Volta, Ghana, Indonesia, the Republic of Northern Yemen and many others. A similar litany of examples would hold true for at least ten of the seventeen historically black land-grant universities.

The nature of involvement over the years has varied, encompassing the following types of activities: (a) institution building, (b) research and research system development, (c) cooperative extension related field activities, (d) degree training at the graduate and undergraduate levels, (e) in-service training through specially designed short-courses, (f) project design and assessment, and (g) policy dialogue and formulation in both the United States and developing countries. While the nature of the work with AID has been varied within and among universities, it has been consistently supported via Cooperative Agreements, contracts and/or grants. In all cases AID has been a major funding partner. Although it should perhaps be noted that over the years (including the recent decade) the historically black land-grant universities have participated in development activities sponsored and funded by other organizations, those activities are not the focus of this paper.

The authors recognize the important educational and economic development roles played by the 1890 institutions in both domestic and international endeavors. There is, in fact, a mutual dependency between the domestic and international initiatives. However, although this is the "centennial year", no attempt has been made to present a discourse on "one hundred years of international involvement." Rather, the focus is on the recent decade during which significant involvement has taken place and for which statistical data is available. It is hoped that this paper will provide insight into the broader spectrum of international involvement by the 1890 land-grant universities.

Impetus for 1890 Institutions' Involvement in International Development

The compelling force which drives the 1890 universities' participation in international development assistance efforts, although complex, can be characterized as made up of both exogenous and endogenous considerations. While these considerations are discussed in a bifurcated context, in this paper, they are felt to be intertwined and, as such, feed upon each other. The endogenous considerations arise out of faculty self-interest, institutional commitment, and a humanitarian need to participate in the national effort to combat hunger, malnutrition, and economic deprivation in the less developed countries (LDCs). The institutions' commitment and response capability result from the concern and commitment of the faculty and administrations. The exogenous considerations can be characterized as the "push" and "pull" toward active involvement. The push/pull impetus come as a result of legislative direction and enablement (Title XII), executive orders, and extra-organizational promotions.

The endogenous response of the 1890 universities, while ultimately feeding upon faculty interest and commitment, is also seen as an institutional reaction to a desire for helping fulfill national and international needs. These needs are discussed next and are followed by sections on legislative and executive direction, and the Cooperative Agreement between the National Association for Equal Opportunity in Higher Education (NAFEO) and AID. Finally, this entire section is closed out with coverage of the institutionally pragmatic reasons for engaging in international development activities.

National and International Needs

The United States has an important stake in the economic progress of LDCs. It has political and security interests and important economic relationships (AID, 1985). For example, 40 percent of our exports go to LDCs and 42 percent of our raw materials and commodities come from these countries. As the community of economically prosperous nations expands, all nations benefit, including the United States.

The U.S. foreign economic assistance program furthers American foreign policy objectives and addresses humanitarian concerns as well.

Established in 1961, AID coordinates U.S. foreign assistance efforts. Economic assistance programs are authorized by Congress under the Foreign Assistance Act. Funds to carry out these programs are appropriated by Congress each year and supported by U.S. foreign assistance aimed at a world in which:

- Average life expectancy is 58 years, compared with 75 in the United States.
- Average annual income in the Third World is $700 compared to over $11,000 in developed countries.
- About 40 percent of those aged 15 and over do not know how to read.
- Three out of five people in the developing world do not have access to adequate and safe water.
- Children under the age of 5 account for more than half of all deaths in developing countries.

The role of economic assistance is to build free, prospering economies necessary for free societies. The problem of poverty can best be solved by conditions for self-sustaining economic growth in all nations. Therefore, AID has emphasized four major thrusts in the U.S. economic assistance programs.

- Use of market forces—to stimulate the growth of market economies and the private sector in developing countries.

- Policy dialogue—to help governments of developing countries reform those policies that inhibit economic growth.

- Institutional building—schools, colleges, training organizations, capital markets, and other institutions are necessary for economic growth in developing countries.

- Technology transfer—a key element in development effort to enable countries to develop their own resources. Research is a critical part of this effort.

AID also conducts humanitarian relief activities in support of those who suffer from calamities such as earthquakes, famine, flood, and drought. Programs are conducted, often together with those of other nations and private, charitable organizations, to quickly alleviate the effects of disaster and reduce human suffering.

Recognizing the important role which U.S. foreign assistance plays, and acknowledging the tremendous amounts of personnel and scientific talent required, the 1890 historically black colleges and universities (HBCUs) have responded to this nation's call for increased involvement. These universities contribute significantly to meeting national and international needs.

U.S. universities are the primary centers for the generation of knowledge and the development of skills essential to the U.S. role in development assistance. The development assistance community, especially the overseas missions of AID, needs to be able to draw upon the scientific community in order to apply the most appropriate and current technical expertise and judgement to planning and program implementation. In response to this need to draw upon the U.S. university community, the Title XII legislation has sought to strengthen capacity and commitment of select U.S. universities.

Title XII of the 1961 Foreign Assistance Act required that in order to prevent famine and establish freedom from hunger, the U.S. would strengthen select universities in program-related agricultural institution development and research. This strengthening has been focused on the land-grant university complex, of which the 1890 HBCUs are an integral and vital part. The continuing rationale is that the strengthening effort would help place the universities in a better position for participating in the U.S. government's development assistance efforts (Long, 1986).

AID, as the United States' lead organization in development assistance, has fostered the enhancement of U.S. land-grant universities and has turned to them to build effective partnership linkages. Some of those links which draw upon the expertise of the 1890 institutions are the Joint Memorandum of Understanding (JMOU), the Strengthening Grant Program (SGP), and the research program especially designed for HBCUs. Goals and scopes of these programs and others are discussed elsewhere in this paper. At this juncture the point to be made is that the U.S. and AID depend heavily on the scientific and technical expertise of the 1890 land-grant universities. Recognition of the important roles that land-grant universities continue to fulfill lead Congress to authorize programs to further develop critical expertise.

Demand for scientific and technical expertise is not the only force which pulls the HBCUs into the foreign assistance arena. Ethnic diversity among foreign assistance teams is necessary in order to recognize the ethnic diversity within the world in which the U.S. seeks to provide developmental and politically stabilizing influence. On this important point, former Secretary of State George P. Schultz (1985) had this to say:

> The quality of our foreign assistance policy and of our representation around the world depends directly on our ability to tap the skills and talents of the best of all segments of American society. Not only is it a matter of simple fairness and equity, but the national interest requires that we have a Foreign Service Officers Corps that represents the rich ethnic diversity of the United States.

> The historically black colleges and universities have a central role to play in this effort and in other areas .... This was recognized by the President's Executive Order 12320, signed back in 1981.

It should be well-understood by observation that the 1890 land-grant universities are undoubtedly the most ethnically diverse of all U.S. universities at both the faculty and student levels. This diversity, coupled with strong scientific and technical capability, places these universities in unique positions to be of continuous and meaningful service to the U.S. diplomatic efforts.

Executive and Legislative Directions

On September 15, 1981, the incumbent president issued Executive Order (EO) 12320 ordering "each Executive Department and those Executive agencies designated by the Secretary of Education" to participate in a "federal program designed to achieve a significant increase in the participation by HBCUs in federally sponsored programs."

On September 22, 1982, the president issued a memorandum for the heads of all executive departments and agencies in emphasis of EO 12320 and directing them: (1) wherever possible to place emphasis on use of program funds to improve the administrative infrastructure of the HBCUs, (2) to increase the *percentage share* of funding for all higher education to be allocated to HBCUs, and (3) to continue efforts to eliminate barriers and to single out policies and regulations which inhibit full participation of HBCUs.

In 1984, the "Gray Amendment" was passed. Though dealing more broadly with achieving the fuller involvement of minority private firms and voluntary agencies as well as HBCUs, it in effect mandated for the HBCUs the same type of emphasis as did the President's directives. The Gray Amendment to the 1984 continuing resolution provided that:

> Except to the extent that the Administrator of the Agency for International Development determines otherwise, not less than 10 percent of the aggregate of the funds made available for the fiscal year 1984 to carry out Chapter 1 of Part 1 of the Foreign Assistance Act of 1961 shall be made available only for activities of economically and socially disadvantaged enterprises (within the meaning of section 133 (c) (5) of the International Development and Food Assistance Act of 1977), historically black colleges and universities, and private and voluntary organizations which are controlled by individuals who are Black Americans, Hispanic Americans, or Native Americans, or who are economically and socially disadvantaged (within the meaning of section 133(c) (5)(B) and (C) of the International Development and Food Assistance Act of 1977). For purposes of this section, economically and socially disadvantaged individuals shall be deemed to include women.

While both the Gray Amendment (1984) and EO 12320 (1981) were in place and operable over a common span of time, the former set forth a more specific target. In fact, the specified target of 10 percent and follow on oversight from the "hill" helped to guide the agency's efforts for increasing HBCU involvement and subsequent funding. EO 12320 has had a more comprehensive impact throughout the agency.

Immediately upon receiving EO 12320, AID took steps to implement it; therefore, some progress was underway with respect to HBCUs by the time the Gray Amendment of 1984 was passed. AID had for some years given special grants to selected HBCUs under special Section 211d (later 122d) and under Title XII authorities. It had long been felt, however, that these grants had not produced the desired result of getting HBCUs adequately involved in normal AID technical assistance and training activities. So, the Bureau for Science and Technology was assigned responsibility for Agency leadership in responding to the HBCU initiatives, for providing liaison with the White House Initiatives Staff, and for preparing required annual plans and annual reports. The Bureau evolved a strategy for carrying out these responsibilities which is outlined below.

The basic strategy of AID has been straightforward.* It has been to expand in a major way the extent of HBCU involvement in regular programs. AID's mission and mandate are to assist LDCs achieve their development aspirations. U.S. colleges and universities have been, historically, a significant source of technical advice and assistance to host countries and to their educational and other development-oriented institutions, primarily by conducting research on major problems impeding their development and by training personnel for their scientific and professional leadership. The basic strategy was designed to increase sharply the participation of the HBCUs in that process.

This basic strategy features expanding the HBCUs' involvement in AID's regular and, therefore, enduring programs of assistance to developing countries, supported by special measures to assist HBCUs carry out this role. This emphasis was designed to avoid the wasting of human and institutional resources involved in preparing institutions for roles which fail to develop.

Building on the basic strategy, the Agency developed a supportive strategy of special assistance grants to selected HBCUs to help them

---

* Excerpted from AID staff documents developed by Dr. Erven J. Long and Science and Technology Bureau/Research and University Relations staff.

achieve an expanded and more effective participation in regular AID programs. These grants are based on assessment of AID's long-term real program needs and are carefully designed to avoid creation of capabilities which are never actually utilized.

Twenty years' experience with long-term "set-aside" grants to HBCUs have demonstrated clearly that such grants accomplish little but mutual frustration unless they are made part of, or closely tied to, arrangements to use these resources in regular assistance programs. To the extent that various types of grants to individual HBCUs are so designed that they lead to and make more effective these institutions' participation in U.S. foreign assistance efforts, they attract and challenge outstanding professional and scientific faculty and provide a sense of worthiness and pride to the institution.

AID's supportive strategy has been implemented through a series of actions. Some of them are:

- Issuing four major directives and guidance documents to Mission Directors and other key executives.

- Awarding a major contract with NAFEO to assist HBCUs increase their involvement in AID programs.

- Establishing a system for providing early notification of program opportunities overseas for HBCUs. This has recently been supplemented by a special description in a single document of all projects which might be implemented in full or in part by an HBCU. This information has been disseminated to HBCUs.

- Issuing a policy directive which, insofar as feasible, shifts AID-funding projects with universities from host country contracting to direct AID contracting—thus removing a major barrier for HBCUs entering into overseas contracts.

- Assigning a senior foreign service officer, full-time, to the task of identifying every possible opportunity and pushing in every way feasible throughout the Agency toward consummation of arrangements for involving HBCUs in country assistance projects and participant training arrangements.

- Providing advice to non-HBCU universities, which have ongoing project relationships with LDCs concerning the advantages of involving an HBCU as a partner in such efforts.

AID's supportive strategy involved two major program elements. The first of these was a special competitive research program open only to HBCUs. The program's purpose was to identify researchers of outstanding talent and, through the quality and usefulness of their research, get them, the field missions, and the developing country personnel mutually acquainted. The second program element was a set of long-term JMOUs between AID and selected pairs of universities, linking an 1890 HBCU with a major university experienced and heavily engaged in AID work. These memoranda incorporate a Program Support Grant—matched in the case of the non-HBCUs with one dollar contributed by the university for each dollar granted by AID. The 1890 universities, however, are required to provide one dollar for every two dollars granted by AID.

Prior to the Gray Amendment and EO 12320, the 1890 HBCU role had been supported by the Title XII Amendment to the Foreign Assistance Act. While Title XII and the associated strengthening grants are not the focus in this paper, it should be noted that legislation has continued to have lasting impact. Not only has it paved the way for present directives and programs, but it has exerted the first clear sign of unambiguous leadership in this area.

The NAFEO/AID Initiative

Over the years, AID has employed several different means to strengthen the capacity of U.S. educational institutions in supporting the Agency's international development programs. One such effort, initiated specifically to strengthen development assistance capacities of HBCUs, has been AID's Cooperative Agreement with NAFEO. The purpose of the agreement is to provide support to NAFEO to utilize its established linkages with the HBCUs to access and make available to AID information regarding institutional and academic capabilities of HBCUs. Specifically, the agreement has used NAFEO to: (1) pinpoint HBCU strengths in AID's priority sectors; (2) coordinate data gathering; (3) conduct information conferences and seminars; and (4) make information available to HBCUs regarding AID's goals, procedures, acquisition regulations, and assistance programs.

NAFEO activities under the agreement include:

- Advising the Agency on general strengths and capabilities of HBCUs and on international development resources available at the over one hundred HBCUs designated as participants.
- Communicating with the HBCUs regarding opportunities for participating in the Agency's acquisition and assistance programs.
- Providing technical assistance to HBCUs in preparation and submission of proposals.
- Acting as HBCU liaison in the data gathering and dissemination processes for individual institutions and scholars.
- Orienting HBCUs to the Agency's overseas research, technical assistance, and training needs.

NAFEO employs a small staff to assist in implementing the Cooperative Agreement. In addition, most of the member schools have designated liaison officers for the AID program.

AID-Related Involvement by 1890 Land-Grant Universities (1979–1989)

Up to this point, information has been presented to show the diverse factors involved in the participation of the 1890 institutions in AID international development activities. We have examined the basic rationale for the involvement of 1890 institutions and why their participation has been critical for the success of AID's Title XII foreign policy initiatives. In this next section, we will look at the nature, extent, type and the geographic focus of AID-funded international development activities undertaken by these Institutions over the past decade, 1979–1989, with specific emphasis on the 1984–1989 period, since reliable pre-1984 data are not easily available.

Although many of the 1890 universities have had a long history of providing technical assistance to developing countries, their effective involvement *as a group* only began with the implementation of the 1975 Title XII legislation—an amendment to the U.S. 1961 Foreign Assistance Act. Title XII was enacted to increase and make more effective the participation of land-grant and other U.S. universities in the U.S. foreign assistance programs. During the period 1978–1985, fifty-nine U.S. universities received Title XII strengthening grants from AID.

Type and Scope of 1890 Involvement in
AID Development Assistance Programs

Section 211(d) Grant Program

Strengthening the capacities of U.S. institutions to help with AID's technical assistance programs did not start with the Title XII legislation of 1975. Prior to Title XII, the Foreign Assistance Act of 1961, as amended, had contained a similar provision. Section 211(d) of Title II had provided funding for "assistance to research and educational institutions in the U.S., for the purpose of strengthening their capacity to develop and carry out programs concerned with the economic and social development of developing countries." A large number of universities, which later became Title XII institutions, were recipients of Section 211(d) grants. Four 1890 universities received 211(d) grants, namely, North Carolina A & T, Southern, Tuskegee, and Virginia State Universities.

Strengthening Grant Program (1979–1985)

Twelve 1890 institutions received non-matching AID strengthening grants over a period of about six years, for a total funding level of about $1.0 million per fiscal year. These funds were given out under Title XII Legislation to strengthen and to make more effective the participation of those schools in the U.S. foreign assistance programs. Forty-seven other U.S. universities received matching strengthening grants from AID over the same period. Table 7.1 gives a listing of the 1890 universities which received strengthening grants.

An assessment of the Strengthening Grant Program reveals that the 1890 universities used these grants for faculty development, administrative capacity development, curriculum development, and research base development. The subject matter focus of these grants was also consistent with the Title XII mandate, as well as with AID demand, namely nutrition, farming systems, crop production/agronomy, livestock (particularly small animals), agricultural education, technology transfer, and women-in-development.

Table 7.1
Supportive AID Grants Received by 1890 Universities.

1890 Institution	211(d) Programs	Strengthening Grant	Program Support Grant
Alabama A & M University		X	X
Alcorn State University		X	
Delaware State University			
Florida A & M University		X	X
Fort Valley State College		X	X
Kentucky State University			
Langston University			
Lincoln University		X	X
North Carolina A & T University	X	X	X
Prairie View A & M University		X	X
South Carolina State University			
Southern University	X		X
Tennessee State University		X	X
Tuskegee University	X	X	X
University of Arkansas—Pine Bluff		X	X
Univ. of Maryland—East Shore		X	X
Virginia State University	X	X	X

X signifies that the university received grant.

Joint Memoranda of Understanding/Program Support Grant (1986-Present)

The JMOUs between AID and selected pairs of U.S. land-grant universities, have provided a basis for the paired universities to utilize their complementary strengths in jointly responding to the needs of developing countries in the areas of food, nutrition, and agricultural development. As indicated earlier, the two universities involved in these JMOUs are an 1890 institution linked with any 1862 land-grant University which is experienced and heavily engaged in AID work. The JMOUs are associated with the Program Support Grant (PSG), matched by both universities, in each case with nonfederal funds.

The JMOU has set forth understandings between AID and the two universities which facilitates the continuity of the universities' involvement and has helped to assure AID of enhanced resources and greater capacity to support AID's Title XII programs. The JMOU has also sought to increase the opportunity for 1890 universities to participate in AID's development programs in agriculture, rural development, and nutrition by pairing them with larger institutions.

Twelve 1890 universities are currently receiving AID funding through the JMOU/PSG. According to AID's original plans in 1985, each 1890 university would receive a PSG of $130,000 annually; however, due to drastic budget reductions, the 1988 level of funding was only approximately $89,000.

HBCU Research Grant Program (1984–1989)

The basic strategy of AID in initiating a Research Grant program for HBCUs has been to expand opportunities for their participation in international technical cooperation programs of the United States government.

For AID, the rationale for the HBCU Research Grant program is straightforward. By offering opportunities for involvement in overseas development activities, the considerable but largely untapped expertise of HBCUs would become better known to officials in developing countries and in AID Missions. In carrying out research programs, HBCU principal investigators would gain valuable experience in addressing problems of developing countries. That expertise would enhance the competitiveness of HBCUs in securing grants and contracts for technical assistance projects from AID and other funding organizations. In addition, more extensive participation by HBCUs in Research and Development would strengthen their overall research instructional programs.

At the outset of the HBCU Research Grants program, AID clearly enunciated a dual purpose: (a) to produce high-quality research, and (b) to assist HBCU institutions in applying their talents to international development problems.

HBCU Research Grants were first awarded in 1984. From fiscal year (FY) 1984 through FY 1989, AID received approximately 450 unsolicited research proposals in the priority program areas of agriculture, nutrition, health, population, natural resources utilization, energy, social sciences, rural development, education, and human resources development. Table 7.2 shows that from 1984 through 1989, 104 of these proposals were received, resulting in grants to 29 HBCUs. Table 7.2 also indicates that to date, fourteen 1890 land-grant universities have been awarded 48 of these research grants.   At the current time the maximum funding for each successful proposal is $100,000.

One of the international agricultural research programs currently funded by AID involves one 1890 institution. This is the Collaborative Research Support Program (CRSP), initiated by AID in 1977. Although ostensibly established to link the capabilities of the U.S. agricultural universities to the needs of developing nations, the CRSP has mainly been reserved for the major U.S. land-grant universities, and to date only one 1890 university, Alabama A & M, is currently involved in one of the eight funded CRSPs—the "Peanut CRSP." The other seven CRSPs are: (1) Bean/Cowpea, (2) Sorghum/Millet, (3) Tropical Soils, (4) Nutrition, (5) Small Ruminants, (6) Pond Dynamics/Aquaculture, and (7) Fisheries.

AID Participant Training Program (1984–1988)

The AID Participant Training Program was a critical element of U.S. foreign assistance. Its primary goal was the development of the human resources potential of citizens of developing countries. Historically, 1890 institutions and other HBCUs have played an important role in training manpower from many of the LDCs. Many of the leaders in these LDCs were trained at the HBCUs, and the experience gained at these institutions has undoubtedly demonstrated to them that the historical experience of training economically disadvantaged groups gives the HBCUs unique insights into the development process. In addition, " . . . the experience of working with low-income rural students and families and the methods HBCU institutions have developed are invaluable resources that should be fully utilized for development efforts in LDCs" (Moland, 1979). The HBCUs have always championed equal opportunity for those denied it or who otherwise could not afford it (Humphries, 1982).

Generally AID funds received by the 1890 universities for Participant Training increased over the five-year period. In addition there was a

Table 7.2
AID Research Program for Historically Black Colleges and Universities.

HBCUs Receiving Grants 1984–1989	Number of Grants
Morehouse College of Medicine	11
Tuskegee University	11
Meharry Medical College	9
Lincoln University	8
Howard University	7
Atlanta University	6
Charles R. Drew Medical School	5
Florida A & M University	5
Morehouse College	5
Fort Valley State College	4
Prairie View A & M University	3
Tennessee State University	3
Texas Southern University	3
Morgan State University	3
South Carolina State University	2
Univ. of Arkansas—Pine Bluff	2
North Carolina A & T State University	2
Alabama A & M University	2
Jackson State College	2
Southern University	2
Benedict College	1
Langston University	1
University of Maryland—Eastern Shore	1
Morris Brown College	1
Philander Smith College	1
Selma College	1
Virginia State University	1
Xavier University	1
Mississippi Valley State	1
TOTAL GRANTS	104
Total Grants to 1890 Institutions	48

fairly close relationship between funding and the number of participants, except in 1986. While the numbers of participants rose dramatically by about 173 percent, from 229 in 1986 to 621 in 1987, there was no corresponding increase in AID funding for this program. Two possible explanations for this anomaly are: (1) differences in the methods used for calculating training costs, and (2) large increases in the number of short-term participants and decreases in the long-term participants.

Since 1986 an average of about 15,000 AID-sponsored participants receive academic or technical training in the U.S. each year. Of this total number, fewer than 3 percent attended 1890 institutions.

AID Contracts and Cooperative Agreements Awarded to 1890 Universities (1984–1988)

Volume of Business. Over the five-year period 1984–1988, the 1890 institutions as a group received a total of approximately $17 million from AID in technical assistance contracts and Cooperative Agreements for international development projects. On an annual basis this is equivalent to an average of $3.4 million for the group. For purposes of comparison, during the three-year period 1981–1983, these universities received only $4.8 million of AID funds for contracts, or an annual average value of $1.6 million.

It is instructive also to compare the level of AID funding received by the 1890 institutions and the twelve PSG-supported 1862 land-grant Universities. The 1862 universities received a total of about $225 million in AID funding for contracts and Cooperative Agreements during the five-year period 1984–1988, or an annual average of $45 million.

Full-Time Equivalents (FTE) for Faculty Involved in AID Development Programs. An analysis of 1890 and 1862 university faculty involvement in AID technical assistance shows the same trend as in the case of volume of business. For the 1890 institutions, the annual average on AID international development activities was about 12 FTEs during the five-year period 1984–1988. For the twelve PSG-supported 1862 universities, the corresponding annual average value was 114 FTEs.

Geographic Focus of 1890 Involvement

The two fundamental requirements for U.S. universities' involvement in AID's Title XII programs have been: (1) the universities must focus their efforts on subject matter areas of direct relevance to AID foreign assistance programs, and (2) the universities must restrict their involvement to AID-designated developing countries.

Table 7.3 shows a listing of countries in which the 1890 universities are currently working on AID-supported project activities. These activities can be simply divided into two groups: (1) research, and (2) technical assistance, the former referring to projects supported under the "HBCU Research Grant Program" (or under the CRSP) and the latter denoting AID-funded contract activities. The areas involved include:

Africa (Sub-Saharan)

Africa (Sub-Saharan) has constituted the geographical region of major focus for the 1890 institutions. All the countries involved are AID-designated developing countries, as evident in table 7.3. It is clear from table 7.3 that the predominant AID-funded type of developing activity pursued by the 1890 universities is "research," with only a few of these institutions involved in AID technical assistance contracts or Cooperative Agreements.

Latin American/Caribbean

Despite the close proximity of the U.S. to Latin America, the 1890 institutions are involved in only a few AID-funded project activities in this region. In addition, despite numerous "linkage" type visits to the region over the past decade by 1890 personnel, few of these visits have resulted in AID-funded programs or projects.

Asia-Near East

Asia-Near East region projects funded by AID and carried out by the 1890 universities have increased significantly in recent years, due in part to important research initiatives by South Carolina State and Tennessee State Universities, and Fort Valley State College.

Table 7.3
Geographic Location of 1890 AID-Funded Development Activities

Regions/Countries	Type of AID Activity	Institutions
Africa:		
Botswana	RES	TSU
Burkina Faso	RES	TU, AAMU
Burundi	TA	LU
Cameroon	TA	UMES, AAMU, FAMU, TU
Guinea	TA	FVSC
Gambia	TA	VSU
Ghana	RES	PVAM, TSU
Kenya	RES	VSU
Liberia	TA	LU
Lesotho	RES	NCAT
Niger	TA, RES	AAMU, TU
Nigeria	RES	TU, AAM
Rwanda	TA	LU, NCAT
Senegal	RES	TU
Sierra Leone	RES	SU, TSU
Swaziland	TA	TSU
Zaire	RES	NCAT
Zambia	RES	UMES, NCAT
Zimbabwe	RES	FVSC
Asia-Near East:		
Bangladesh	TA	LU
India	RES	FVSC
Indonesia	TA	UAPB
Philippines	RES	SCSU
Nepal	TA, RES	VSU, FVSC
Thailand	RES	SCSU
Latin America/Caribbean:		
Belize	TA, RES	SU, LU
Barbados	RES	LU
Dominican Republic	RES, TA	FVSC

Table 7.3 continued.
Geographic Location of 1890 AID-Funded Development Activities

Regions/Countries	Type of AID Activity	Institutions
Haiti		
	RES, TA	FAMU, TU
Jamaica	TA, RES	SU, LU, TU, FAMU
Peru	RES	FAMU

Key:
   Type of Activity:
TA   Technical Assistance (Contract, Cooperative Agreement)
RES   Research Grant (mostly "HBCU—Research Grant Program")
   Institutions:

AAMU	Alabama A & M University	SCSU	South Carolina State University
TSU	Tennessee State University	FVSC	Fort Valley State College
FAMU	Florida A & M University	TU	Tuskegee University
LU	Lincoln University	UAPB	University of Arkansas—Pine Bluff
NCAT	North Carolina A & T University	UMES	University of Maryland—Eastern Shore
VSU	Virginia State University	PVAM	Prairie View A & M University
SU	Southern University		

United States

The HBCU Research Grant Program has supported collaborative-type research between outstanding HBCU scientists and collaborators in the LDCs on topics of mutual interest and importance. Depending upon the nature of the investigation conducted, most of the more basic-type research have usually been carried out on the campuses of 1890 universities. The benefits of this AID-funded research program to the 1890 institutions have been considerable, and it is not inaccurate to state that the major portion of these funds are spent in the United States, targeted on improving research capacity in the HBCUs.

Future Involvement: Impetus and Prospects

In order to properly understand the involvement of 1890 universities (and HBCUs in general) in AID's development assistance programs, one must appreciate that: (1) the HBCUs are a viable resource to use, and (2) HBCUs have a rich history of working with many LDCs. In addition, the involvement of 1890 universities has been mandated by AID through numerous support-type grants—211(d), Strengthening, Program Support and "HBCU Research Grant." However, as the data presented above indicates (Type and Scope of 1890 Involvement, p. 79), only modest increases in the participation of 1890 institutions in the Agency's programs during the past decade have been noted. The total dollar figure of $43.1 million for all years amounts to less than 10 percent of funding awarded to the 1862 land-grant universities. There are undoubtedly numerous factors responsible for this. In this section we will briefly examine some of these issues as well as look at future prospects for the 1890 universities in AID's international program activities.

Perhaps the most overriding factor to be addressed in discussing the 1890 institutions involvement (or lack of involvement) in AID's programs is the fact the there are very limited faculty resources in the 1890 universities which can readily be mobilized for AID's international development activities. While there are outstanding competencies within individual departments at the 1890 universities, institutionally there is no excess or "surplus capacity" that can respond with immediacy to AID's demands. Thus in any analysis, 1890 institutions' participation in AID international projects reveals a low ceiling for the volume of overseas technical assistance (FTEs) which the 1890 universities can provide to AID. However, this level would seem not to have been reached yet. Currently, the average annual FTEs supplied by the 1890 institutions numbers only about twelve; however, the 1890 universities as a group could supply two or three times that level without any sacrifice in the quality or quantity of their domestic programs.

The Title XII legislation, enacted in 1975, envisioned an expanding role for U.S. universities working in partnership with AID to address food-related problems in developing countries. A recent U.S. Government Accounting Office (GAO) Report (April 1989), indicates that during the seven-year period 1975–1982, the total number of new Title XII-type contracts and grants for technical assistance to developing countries, increased significantly, reaching a peak in 1982. Since 1982, however, the number of new Title XII-type projects awarded each year has declined by more than one-half. Furthermore, the GAO Report indicates that by the end of FY 1990, approximately 75 percent of the 142 ongoing Title XII-type projects will have terminated. Since 1981–1982 the U.S. Congress has directed AID to make fuller use of Private

Voluntary Organizations and private sector firms to implement international development projects. These initiatives have further contributed to the decline in Title XII project activity.

There is concern at some 1890 institutions about the universities' ability to continue to maintain international development capability in the light of the drastic decline in the volume of AID projects awarded to the universities. Furthermore, many universities are finding it increasingly more difficult to encourage faculty to learn foreign languages and to maintain interest in international work when the opportunities for working overseas dwindle with each passing year.

In the area of participant training, there is no doubt that the 1890 institutions as a group can certainly provide appropriate training for many more trainees than they currently do. At present, fewer than 3 percent of the total number of participant trainees entering the U.S. are placed at 1890 institutions. However, there are certain historical factors that tend to operate against the placement of large numbers of participant trainees at HBCUs.

In many LDCs, potential participant trainees have traditionally been convinced to believe that "up-to-date state-of-the-art" training can only be obtained in the U.S. at large prestigious universities. While this is perhaps true for some post-graduate and specialized-type training, it is certainly not true for basic undergraduate training, as the 1890 universities and many HBCUs offer programs at the undergraduate level comparable with most larger institutions. However, this perception of the 1890 institutions still persists in many countries—as excellence in providing training is often associated with traditional prestigious schools as well as with internationally famous scholars residing at these institutions. While the above state of affairs has changed drastically in recent years, it still continues to have negative impact on the numbers of participants placed at 1890 universities by AID Missions and host countries.

It would seem that the HBCUs as a group need to adopt appropriate aggressive strategies which will significantly improve their procuring more AID contracts and grants, as well as more participant trainees. In this regard it is significant to note that NAFEO, in an attempt to better market the competencies and image of the HBCUs as a group, has recently developed a comprehensive brochure giving a capability-profile of these institutions. Copies of this brochure are to be sent to

AID Missions and to host country institutions and governments. In addition, some of the AID-funded JMOU/PSG University partners have developed brochures describing their joint approach toward international technical assistance. Copies of these have been distributed to AID Mission personnel and officials in LDCs.

Summary

While 1890 universities' involvement in AID development programs has fluctuated from year to year, it has increased only modestly over the past five years with a slight peak in 1987. Participant Training and Technical Assistance contracts account for about 80 percent of total AID funds received by the 1890 institutions. However, when compared to the larger 1862 land-grant universities, the participation of 1890 universities in AID's programs is marginal.

The future prospects for participation by 1890 institutions (and indeed all U.S. universities) in AID's Title XII programs are not bright. In recent years there has been a drastic reduction in the number of Title XII-designated projects, due in part to an interplay of factors such as changing congressional and AID priorities, budgetary concerns, reluctance of some AID personnel to use 1890 institutions, and continuing negative perception of these universities' performance in implementing AID development programs.

References

Agency for International Development. *Annual Performance Reports for Historically Black Colleges and Universities.* Washington, D.C.: Agency for International Development, 1983–87.

——. "Supporting Agricultural Research Faculties of Agriculture in Africa." Washington, D.C., April 11, 1985.

——. "Science and Technology in the Agency for International Development." Washington, D.C., 1988.

——. *An Assessment of A.I.D. Activities to Promote Agricultural and Rural Development in Sub-Sahara Africa.* AID Evaluation Special Study No. 54, Washington, D.C., 1988.

——. *Economic Growth and The Third World: A Report on The AID Private Enterprise Initiative.* Washington, D.C., 1988.

———. Office of Research Science and Technology Bureau. "Guidelines for Submitting Proposals Under the HBCU Research Program." Washington, D.C.: Agency for International Development, 1987.

Brand, Jean. *Title XII and BIFAD: Helping A Hungry World Feed Its Own.* Washington, D.C.: NASULGC and BIFAD, 1981.

Humphries, Frederick. "A Perspective on 1890 Institutions' Participation in International Agricultural Development." Address presented at Conference of the Association of U.S. Directors of International Agricultural Programs, University of Nebraska, June 8–10, 1982.

Mellor, John W. "From Hunger to Food Aid to Commercial Markets." Remarks before a Joint AID/Winrock International Workshop, February 21, 1989.

Moland, John. "Social Cultural and Economic Characteristics of the Clientele." In *The Unique Resources of 1890 Institutions*, edited by T.T. Williams, pp. 15–21. Baton Rouge, Louisiana: Louisiana State University Printing Office, 1979.

National Association for Equal Opportunity in Higher Education. *Institutional and Presidential Profiles of NAFEO's 117 HBCUs*, vol. 9. Washington, D.C.: National Association for Equal Opportunity in Higher Education, April, 1989.

National Association of State Universities and Land-Grant Colleges, International Affairs Division. *Basic Principles of College and University Involvement in International Development Activities*. Washington, D.C.: NASULGC, 1984.

Rayburn, W. G. "A Perspective on Internationalizing the College Curriculum." Speech presented before an Annual Meeting of Association of Agricultural Administrators, Washington, D.C., April, 1989.

Schultz, George P. *Foreign Policy and The Black Community*. Current Policy No. 680. Washington, D.C.: U.S. Department of State, Bureau of Public Affairs, 1985.

Thompson, Robert L. "Development Assistance, Trade Policies, and Farm Programs: The Interconnections." Remarks at a Joint AID/Winrock International Workshop, Washington, D.C., January 1989.

U.S. General Accounting Office Report. "Foreign AID Issues Concerning U.S. University Participation." Report to the Committee on Foreign Affairs, House of Representatives. Washington, D.C.: U.S. Government Printing Office, April 1989.

Williamson, H., Jr. "Planning and Coordination of Federally Funded Research at 1890 Land-Grant Universities." Testimony to the U.S. House Sub-Committee on Operations, Research, and Foreign Agriculture. *The Congressional Record*. Serial No. 98-30 (1983), pp. 403–413.

Williamson, H., Jr. "The 1890 Universities at Crossroads: Changing Times. Shifting Support and a Future of Challenge." Address before the Farm Home and Minister's Institute, Tennessee State University, Nashville, Tennessee, 1987.

Williamson, H., Jr. "Internationalization of Research Programs: Problems and Concerns for the 1890 Land-Grant Universities." Paper presented to the Association of Agricultural Administrators Annual Meeting, Washington, D.C., April 1989.

Williamson, H., Jr. and T.T. Williams. "Teaching, Research and Extension Programs at Predominantly Black Land-Grant Universities." *Southern Journal of Agricultural Economics* 17 (1985), pp. 31–41.

Williams, T.T. *The Unique Resources of 1890 Land-Grant Institutions.* Baton Rouge, Louisiana: Louisiana State University Press, 1979.

Williams, T.T. and Handy Williamson, Jr. "Teaching, Research and Extension Programs at Historically Black (1890) Land-Grant Universities." *Journal of Agriculture History*, 1988.

Woods, Alan. "Food and Agriculture Goals, Directions and Operations for the 1990s." Remarks before a Joint AID/Winrock International Workshop, Washington, D.C., June 4, 1989.

PART III

The Future Role of
1890 Institutions

Hydroponics Experiment with Sweet Potatoes Project (School of Agricultural Sciences, TuskegeeUniversity, Tuskegee, Alabama, and NASA). Susanne Loomis, Photographer.

8

Future Roles of 1890 Land-Grant Institutions: Instruments of Opportunity and Excellence

Benjamin F. Payton

The preconference's focus is on the challenges and opportunities of the 1890 Land-Grant Institutions and Tuskegee University. It is ironic and somewhat paradoxical that this meeting should occur just after the announcement of a new court decision that could have the effect of dismantling the largest of the 1890 institutions, namely, Southern University where we meet here in Baton Rouge, Louisiana. This decision has received considerable attention already today. However, in order to talk about the future, we must proceed on the basis of an adequate understanding of how the past has shaped the present. Aristotle, a Greek philosopher who lived from 384 to 322 before Christ, put it this way: "When studying problems we begin with causes." It is essential to remember that the creation of Black institutions was not the *cause* of racial inequality and discrimination, and neither will their elimination be the cure. As we consider the role of 1890 Institutions in the years ahead, we must keep in mind that we are members of the national system of higher education. For this reason, we cannot function in a vacuum, but rather as a part of the system.

Consequently, to discuss the future role of the 1890 Land-Grant Institutions, the first question to answer is, Who are they? It is particularly important to note that this question of identity and mission continues to be raised in many places in the United States, even at a time when the 1890 Land-Grant Institutions have been firmly established in more than a third of the states for one hundred years.

In dealing with definitions, let us consider first the land-grant college system. Senator Justin Smith Morrill introduced the first land-grant bill in 1859. However, it was vetoed by President James Buchanan. Senator Morrill introduced the land-grant bill again in 1862.

> It proposed that portions of federally owned land be sold and the proceeds used for the "perpetual endowment" in each State of at least one college whose main aim would be, without excluding other scientific and classical studies, and including military tactics, to teach such branches of learning as are related to agriculture and the mechanic arts in such a manner as the legislatures of the states may respectively subscribe, in order to promote the liberal and practical education of the industrial classes in the several pursuits and professions of life.

This bill was enacted by the Congress, signed by President Lincoln July 2, 1862, and became the foundation of our land-grant college system, including both the 1862 and the 1890 institutions.

The question regarding 1890 institutions must be answered in several stages as follows:

1. In retrospect—1890–1965.
2. Current status—1965–1989.
3. In the years ahead—1990 and beyond.

In Retrospect

When the land-grant act was passed in 1862, there was legal separation of the races in the seventeen southern states including Alabama, Arkansas, Delaware, Florida, Georgia, Kentucky, Louisiana, Maryland, Mississippi, Missouri, North Carolina, Oklahoma, South Carolina, Tennessee, Texas, Virginia, West Virginia (no longer functioning as an 1890 Institution state).

Thus, the Black Americans residing in the seventeen southern states did not have access to the land-grant system during the period 1862–1890. In 1890, Congress passed a second Morrill Act that was designed to provide additional funds to support instruction in the 1862 institutions.

A provision was included, however, that these 1890 land-grant funds would not be available to states which did not admit Black Americans to the land-grant institutions. This concept was circumvented by acceptance of the concept of "separate-but-equal." Out of all this came the 1890 Land-Grant Institutions. So, the initial role of the 1890 Land-Grant Institutions was to extend the benefits of the 1862 Land-Grant Act to Black Americans in the states having legal segregation of the races. Just as in the case of the 1862 Institutions, the basic mission of the 1890 Institutions included instruction, research, and service. For the next seventy-five years (1890–1965) the 1890 Institutions functioned admirably on limited resources from state and private sources. During this period of seventy-five years, the federal government did not provide a single dime of formula funds to the historically black institutions.

Current Status

The decade of the 1960s ushered in a period of rude awakening to the inhumanity and devastation of the practices of racial discrimination. Black Americans themselves rose up against the practice, and the larger society, including the federal government, began to take open and visible steps to ultimately eliminate the ravages of racial discrimination.

In 1965, Public Law 89-106 was passed by the Congress to provide the U.S. Secretary of Agriculture with a discretionary appropriation of $2 million. Beginning in 1967, $283, 000 was taken from this fund and divided among the 1890 Institutions on the basis of a newly established formula. This represents the beginning of formula funding of agricultural programs at the 1890 Institutions. This funding has increased over the years such that the total account for the period 1967 through 1990, based on the current projections, stands at $685,500,000.

In addition to the significant funding which occurred over the past twenty-five years, many progressive developments have occurred in the larger society, led especially by the federal government, to bring the 1890 Institutions functionally into the community of land-grant education. It suffices here to briefly mention some of the developments without extensive elaboration and not necessarily in chronological order. Some of those which immediately come to mind include:

- The National Association of State Universities and Land-Grant Colleges (NASULGC) openly admitted and encouraged membership in the Association by the 1890 Institutions, including full participation in the Department of Agriculture.

- The 1890 Institutions enjoy full and active membership and participation in some of the major policy groups associated with NASULGC and United States Department of Agriculture (USDA) including:

  - the Extension Committee on Organization and Policy (ECOP)

  - the Experiment Station Committee on Organization and Policy (ESCOP)

  - the Resident Instruction Committee on Organization and Policy (RICOP)

  - the International Committee on Organization and Policy (ICOP)

- Under executive instructions, more than fifty federal departments and agencies have identified within their own ranks a person responsible for identifying and facilitating the involvement of the 1890 Institutions in the benefits of the respective federal units.

- In 1988, the USDA conducted a very high-level forum in Nashville, Tennessee, designed to strengthen and expand the work of the 1890 Institutions. Out of it has come some very significant activities, including the establishment and staffing of a liaison position and office on each 1890 campus.

- In the decade of the 1980s, three presidents of the United States have paused to issue Executive Orders (EOs) in support of, among others, the 1890 Land-Grant Institutions:

  - President Jimmy Carter

    in order to overcome the effects of discriminatory treatment, and to strengthen and expand the capacity of the historically black colleges and universities . . . . (EO 12232, August 8, 1980)

  - President Ronald Reagan

    to strengthen the capacity of the historically black colleges and universities to provide quality education and to overcome the effects of discriminatory treatment . . . . (EO 12320, September 15, 1981)

- President George Bush

  to strengthen the capacity of historically black colleges and universities to provide quality education, and to increase opportunities to participate in the benefits of federal programs . . . . (EO 12677, April 28, 1989)

These several developments have served to raise the hopes, aspirations, and expectations of the 1890 colleges and universities. The 1890 Institutions are no longer destined or restricted to serving needs of the people left behind for whatever reason—racial, social, economic, or otherwise. We are now members of the National Association of Land-Grant Institutions and destined to serve the needs of the people of the world.

In The Years Ahead

Now that it is firmly established, and recognized, by us and by the nation, that we are members of the national land-grant system, we are duty bound to perform accordingly. Further, we have every right to expect support at the local, state, and national levels commensurate with this recognition.

In response to developments over the last twenty-five years, we have organized ourselves into the Council of 1890 Presidents and other administrative groups to take full advantage of the opportunities which have emerged. This means moving on the basis of national goals and priorities established for the national system. ECOP has established national goals and priorities for extension, ESCOP has established national initiatives for research, and RICOP has established national initiatives for instruction.

These policy statements have been published and widely distributed; therefore, they are not repeated here. It suffices to say, however, that these policies, with respect to projections, will serve the 1890 Institutions just as the rest of the land-grant system.

One big addition must be added to the broad policy and program projections stated above. In spite of the commitment of the 1890

Institutions to comply with the national initiatives, they have an additional duty and responsibility to go beyond the customary horizon in reaching and serving the minorities. This mission may involve a national awareness campaign designed broadly for public consumption, but with a major focus on youth in grades K through 12. In addition, 1890 Institutions have a major responsibility to develop programs to enroll and retain minorities in college. The pool of minorities for employment in advanced scientific, technological, and professional positions is rapidly diminishing. This emphasizes the need for 1890 Institutions to make graduate education a very high priority for the years ahead.

When Booker T. Washington started Tuskegee in 1881, July 4, there were no buildings, no land, no land-grant, no equipment, no faculty. What he did find were "hundreds of hungry, earnest souls," as he put it, "who wanted to secure knowledge." The need was great! The deprivation and lack of education that had been forced on the African slaves in America had taken its toll. The African American population, just sixteen years out of slavery, was living in wretched poverty and ignorance. Booker T. Washington observed, in his many trips to visit his potential clientele, that fat pork and cornbread were the mainstay diet. Cotton was planted up to the door steps of their one-room shanties. Gardens were lacking, yet scarce funds were used for frivolities like showy and costly clocks (that didn't keep accurate time), or an unused sewing machine or musical organ. The common day for the entire family was spent in the field planting, chopping, or picking cotton. The cotton crops were usually mortgaged and the people were in debt.

Many things have changed in many ways since 1881. During the last one hundred years, 570,000 graduates have been produced from the 1890 Land-Grant Institutions and Tuskegee University who *were* and *are* great leaders, physicians, inventors, scientists, teachers, and workers who have done great things, individually and collectively for this nation and world. Despite the changes and accomplishments, the description of the rural South, so pictorially described by Booker T. in 1882, is in many ways with new nuances still existing today—yes, over one hundred years later. The poverty, the poor housing, the inadequate diets, the inadequate education, the lack of motivation, the debt still exist. The list goes on and has been expanded: single-parent households, teenage pregnancy, and new twists such as pesticide contamination in food and water, and drugs, to name a few. It is ironic that projections for the twenty-first century indicate that one-third of the work force and 40 percent of school age children will be Blacks and Hispanics. Some 85 percent of the projected new entrants to the work force will be Blacks, Hispanics, and women. The Black population in Alabama averages 25 percent of the population and is up to 90 percent in some of the Black Belt counties. Here resides a greatly unused, wasted, human potential. But they exist almost as foreign enclaves or internal colonies in the United States. To remedy such requires that, in order for the US to remain competitive, it had better educate *all* of its people, especially Blacks and Hispanics, to be skilled laborers, technicians, managers, engineers, and scientists.

In other words, we have come full circle. After one hundred years of "toiling in the vineyard" with scarce resources, the 1890 Institutions and Tuskegee University are needed more than ever. In Booker T.'s day, skills such as farming and brick masonry and blacksmithing were required; now the skills needed are engineering, veterinary medicine, science and math teaching skills, English and foreign language skills, agriculture and food science, natural and environmental sciences, natural resource management, business management, social sciences and family sciences, economics. But the goals are the same: to train African American professionals, to educate disadvantaged and uneducated youth and adults, and in many cases, to retrain workers and adults for second careers or career advancement; all must be educated for life-long learning. Booker T.'s students were young and old. Many of his first students were over forty years old and a number were former teachers. Likewise, in coming years the young and the old will need access to higher education.

What is the future for the 1890 Institutions and Tuskegee University? We can envision:

- Centers of Excellence for educating scientists, managers, educators, professionals needed for enhancing the nation's competitiveness.

- Centers of Excellence in selected fields of engineering, natural and environmental sciences, social sciences, agricultural and food sciences, natural resource management, business management, veterinary medicine, human medicine, nutrition and health, and rural development.

- Centers of Excellence in continuing education and outreach activities to the disadvantaged, the poor, the elderly, single parents, and youth at risk.

This vision mandates that 1890 Institutions and Tuskegee University be intimately involved in the national issues and initiatives to develop a more competitive economy, to improve water quality, to understand food, diet and health relationships, and to manage germ plasm and maintain genetic diversity. Our 1890 institutions must remain an integral part of new discoveries and applications in important plants and animals, improved management of crop pests and diseases and methods of food processing. We must become more involved in plant genome and animal genome research. We must participate in evaluating the impact of climate shifts on agricultural and ecological systems and the impact of these systems on the climate. We must combine research and outreach activities in forest research and productivity, rural development and revitalization, alternative farming methods and biocontrol of pests, and family well-being. We must be involved in the exploration of space and the oceans, and in international and domestic trade policy development.

This vision requires, as stated by John Patrick Jordan on the occasion of the Hatch Centennial that:

> curricula will place more emphasis on interdisciplinary approaches to solving real world problems. There will be much greater flexibility in program design and curriculum. Computer-based programs and self-paced laboratories will be common, leaving more time for student-faculty interaction. The average citizen will have greater access to higher education. Industry, universities, and government will have more interaction, with the university addressing fundamental knowledge and the industrial sector translating new knowledge into economic growth. Scientific literacy will be a basic requirement.

According to Cheikh Anta Diop, the renowned Senegalese anthropologist, linguist, and scientist, *the problem posed by modern man is the pursuit of science with conscience.* The 1890 Institutions and Tuskegee University, and their sister Historically Black Colleges and Universities, are institutions that are entering the twenty-first century poised to lead new efforts that combine science, education and conscience in new ways, and if provided with adequate resources necessary to achieve their full potential, will be significant agencies in the nation's long-term salvation.

9

Widening the Base of the Triangle: What the 1890 Institutions and Tuskegee Institute Have Done and Must Continue to Do

Huel D. Perkins

It is generally agreed that the history of higher education in this country begins with the founding of Harvard University in 1636. It is our oldest example of the attempt in this country to train the minds of our youth beyond that of high school. No doubt, that this experiment if we wish to call it so, has been a success. When this institution celebrated its three hundred fiftieth anniversary some few years ago, it could point to the number of presidents it had produced, the number of governors it had trained, the number of senators and representatives it had spawned, the number of Nobel Prize winners it had nurtured, and the number of Pulitzer Prize winners it had inspired. The list was imposing. This institution had seemingly justified the purpose for which it was founded.

What we also know is that this "experiment" at Harvard and those which followed—the Yales, the Princetons, the Dartmouths—was designed for the sons of the clergy, the sons of the upper crust, the "haves" as opposed to the "have-nots." We know that the education received at these institutions was classical as opposed to practical. We know that these institutions were restrictive in terms of admissions policies, prohibitive in terms of tuition costs, and limited in terms of scope and mission. These institutions, patterned after the European system, prepared a small group of men for law, medicine, theology, and teaching but neglected the education of the vast majority of men and women who belonged to the working class.

As the concept of democracy grew, so did the idea as to what kind of education was needed for this new country. Fortunately, there have always been men and women who dream—men and women who are not afraid to take first steps down uncharted roads with nothing but their visions to guide them. There are some names who are well-known to you who gather here today, for they figure prominently in the history of the land-grant idea and particularly in the history of the 1890 colleges and Tuskegee.

Let me recall two names which are intimately associated with this new idea—this idea which I like to call "widening the base of the triangle." For indeed, they saw the need to make the base of the triangle broader so that more men and women could ascend to the apex of the triangle through education.

The first is that of a Johnathan Baldwin Turner, a graduate of Yale University and a professor at Illinois College who felt strongly that it was possible to educate the masses. In his speeches and articles he advocated that there should be schooling for the working man, that a student should be given the prerogative to choose his own course of study, and that institutional experimentation and research should be conducted for the benefit of the community. The second well-known name associated with land-grant colleges is that of Justin Smith Morrill of Vermont. It was he who introduced a bill in Congress in 1857 to establish a new type of college. It was he who reintroduced the bill after it had narrowly passed Congress in 1859—only to be vetoed by President James Buchanan on the grounds that it was costly and unconstitutional. It was his name which became attached to the act when it was signed into law on July 2, 1862, by President Abraham Lincoln during the darkest days of the Civil War. It was his name which is attached to the act which created the black land-grant colleges and Tuskegee.

Was this concept opposed? Of course it was. Every new ideal of consequence has been met with opposition. Every new invention was opposed. As a favorite novelist of mine tells me: the first motor was considered foolish. The first airplane was considered impossible, the power loom vicious, anesthesia sinful. But thanks to these early pioneers, a concept was advanced and we who sit here today are the beneficiaries of this bold new idea. For without this original concept, the 1890 colleges and Tuskegee would not have come into existence, and we would not be on the eve of celebrating the one hundredth year of these institutions which have virtually changed the face of this nation.

The history of this nation is fraught with instances of dehumanization, denial, and dastardly treatment with regard to minorities—blacks in particular. Especially is this to be noted in the field of education. It is no small wonder that education was used as a tool, for it is generally known that to keep a man enslaved, deny him the opportunity to train his mind. This was never more apparent than in the Black Codes which abounded before the Civil War and thereafter. Blacks could not gather together in a group without a white person being present; they could not bear firearms; they could not enter into contracts; they could not purchase land. But the most devastating of these codes was this: Do not teach slaves how to read and to write. As a race of people, we are still paying for this wretched imposition. When we were emancipated in 1863, there we were—4 million black people with nowhere to go and nothing to do. We were uneducated. We had freedom and nothing else. We had not been allowed to fulfill our purposes as human beings.

Enter the 1890 land-grant colleges and Tuskegee. And we must be forever thankful that they came into existence. For as W. E. B. DuBois writes:

> Southern whites would not teach Negroes. Northern whites in sufficient numbers could not be had. If the Negro was to learn, he must teach himself, and the most effective help that could be given him was the establishment of schools to train teachers . . . without consultation or systematic planning there arose a series of institutions designed to furnish teachers for the untaught . . . in a single generation they put 30,000 black teachers in the South; they wiped out illiteracy for the majority of the black people in the land, and they made Tuskegee possible.

The 1890 colleges were born out of this kind of climate. The Second Morrill Act required that states practicing racial segregation create black colleges as a precondition to receiving funds—from this came the succession of land-grant colleges from Lincoln University in Missouri in 1866, through Alcorn State University in 1871, through South Carolina State College in 1872, on through to the establishment of Tennessee State University in 1909.

What have these institutions wrought? As we stand here today to consolidate our gains and look to the future of these institutions, let us see where they fit in the scheme of American education.

In the chapter entitled "Genesis of the 1890 Institutions and Tuskegee Institute" in the book by Mayberry (1976), *Development of Research at Historically Black Land-Grant Institutions*, appears this paragraph:

> In the early years of the Negro institutions, there was essentially no commonality with respect to either the content or the level of program offerings. The academic programs at these institutions were variously described as elementary, secondary, normal and general education—a few indicated Agriculture, Home Economics, and the Mechanic Arts. The most common purpose of these institutions was for "the training of Negro teachers."

The preparing of teachers seems to me to still be a pressing need of these 1890 land-grant colleges and Tuskegee Institute. The alarming rate of decline among teachers means that this concern must not be abdicated as a mission of these colleges. Let me share a few statistics:

- In 1986, over 43 percent of blacks attending college were enrolled in two-year colleges, many in terminal programs.

- Fewer black students are preparing for teaching careers, even at the 1890 colleges which have traditionally produced more than half of all black teachers. In 1986, the percentage of first-year students intending to major in education dropped from 13.4 percent to 8.7 percent.

- Black children constitute 16 percent of the nation's elementary and secondary school population, while only 6.9 percent of the nation's teachers are black.

- A 1986 report entitled *A Nation Prepared*, by the Carnegie Forum on Education and Economy, projects that by 1990 only 5 percent of the nation's school teachers will be black.

- A 1986 assessment by the American College Testing Program found that teaching not only comes in behind careers in other fields, but also loses out to undecided.

- In the entire state of Michigan, there are only 11 black male teachers between the ages of 21 and 26.

We still need teachers. These institutions must produce them. There is no alternative.

Applied or mission-oriented research, designed to benefit the people of the states of these various institutions, must be continued. As the book *Development of Research at Historically Black Land-Grant Institutions* reported (Mayberry, 1971), a variety of research projects were taking place on these campuses. Developments were progressing in animal science, human nutrition, rural development, and plant and soil science at Lincoln University, Alcorn State University, Florida A & M University, Virginia State University—to list but a few. This must be continued as a mission of these institutions. But, these institutions must also produce graduate students who are equipped to engage in such research. Again, let me cite some sobering statistics:

- The U. S. college-age population has declined since 1979 and will continue to shrink through 1996. Interest in technical careers continues to drop.

- Blacks and Hispanics are 20 percent of the U.S. population but earn fewer than 3 percent of doctoral degrees in science and engineering.

- Only 1 out of every 420 American Ph.D.'s is black.

- More than three times as many graduate degrees are conferred on non-resident aliens than black Americans.

- There are less than 150 holders of the Ph.D. degree in pure mathematics among blacks, living or dead.

- Black undergraduate enrollments declined significantly between 1980 and 1987, while Hispanic and Asian enrollments increased at both undergraduate and graduate level.

- Asians continue to be the only minority group which is over-represented in enrollments and degrees earned at all levels of higher education.

- A report in the *Chronicle of Higher Education* (December 9, 1987) said that more and more black men are choosing *not* to go to college. There is a decline at every level of higher education among black males.

The questions to be asked at this point are these: Who will continue this research mission of the 1890 colleges? Is our supply of researchers dwindling? What must we do about it?

Finally, let us look at the third mission of these colleges, which is service. These institutions have been at the forefront of rendering services directly to those people who needed it through extension agents, short courses and continuing education. There is no doubt in my mind that this aspect of the land-grant colleges must continue. Again, let me cite some statistics which give clear indication that there is still much to do, and that these institutions must be called upon to do it.

- Studies tell us that minority children are beginning to drop out of school as early as the elementary grades. They do so because an older brother or sister has already done so.

- We have been told of 10- and 11-year-olds coming to school in $100 tennis shoes and fur coats and gold chains bought with money received for delivering drugs from one place to another. The beeper had become a status symbol at some elementary schools. Many school systems have not made them illegal on the school grounds.

- Last year, one-half of all babies born in this country were born to teenage girls. Children cannot rear children. If we don't do something about this, the babies will not be the only ones crying in this country. We will all have something to cry about.

- The July 17, 1989 issue of *Time Magazine*, in a feature article, reported that 464 persons had died by hand guns in the space of one week. Many were drug-related; many were suicides.

- More than one-half of all black children live in single-parent homes. One out of every twelve black children lives with neither parent.

Helping people to live more fully than they otherwise would have lived must remain the purpose of all of us. There is the old adage: give a man a fish and you feed him for a day; teach him to fish and you feed him for life. We must somehow reach the masses of this nation and show to them the benefits which accrue to one who is educated. We must stand toe-to-toe with the dope pushers and compete for the minds of our youth. Our institutions must accept the sordid facts of life as challenges for the years ahead. They must serve, but they must serve where it will made a difference in the quality of life of as many people as possible.

My thesis is that the base of the triangle has been widened with the advent of the 1890 land-grant colleges and Tuskegee. They helped this nation move from an education which was restrictive and elitist and designed for white males to one which included women, members of all classes and strata, the sons and daughters of working people—and particularly to one which educated members of minority ethnic and racial groups. This is remarkable, and it is an idea from which America, though reluctant at first to embrace it, has received rich and rewarding dividends. The world needs what is being done in land-grant colleges because there is no other entity presently doing what these institutions do. The world needs your solutions to problems which can be replicated in Third World countries. The world needs the fruits of the basic research which has transpired in these 1890 institutions. The world needs these institutions, which can touch the lives of the students and have them aspire to become involved in the professions, in government, in research, in politics—all of which require a higher education. As Dr. Samuel Proctor reminds us, "Time has not permitted the development of a black social class that is really unfamiliar with poverty and the black ghetto subculture. Even most professional blacks today have parents who were domestics or farm hands . . . . Blacks are one generation from a condition close to slavery." And we should never forget that it was slavery which brought these institutions into existence in the first place.

The base of the triangle has been widened. There is still much to be done. Through scholarship programs, through counseling, through persuasion, through threats, if need be, we must find ways to ensure that youngsters remain in school and then go on to these colleges. We must reverse the trends which indicate that minorities are no longer interested in pursuing advanced degrees or no longer engaged in significant research to improve the lot of our people. We must include the social problems which plague us as a people as a main agenda item for the years ahead. Essentially, these 1890 institutions must continue to distinguish themselves in teaching, research, and service, but with a renewed commitment and a new sense of the problems which we face in this country today.

The base of the triangle has been widened. It now becomes our responsibility to see that as many as are capable climb up the sides of the triangle to its apex. That is what America is all about—allowing an individual to ascend as high as he can in a country which professes to be honest, just, decent, moral, and democratic.

I close with a little story concerning a balloon seller at a carnival. It seems that the vendor had balloons of various colors which he had injected with helium, allowing them to soar skyward when released. He cut a red balloon and it went up into the atmosphere, then next a white balloon, and then next a yellow one. All went quickly up as they were released. A small black boy watching this operation moved over to the vendor and asked this question: "Mister, if you cut that black balloon loose, would it go as high as the others?" The vendor cut the balloon and it, too, soared skyward, whereupon he said to the lad: "You see, it goes as high as the others. It is not the color of the balloon on the outside which makes it rise, it's the stuff on the inside."

These institutions must continue to put "stuff on the inside" which permits its students to rise to the apex of this triangle which was widened with the establishment of the 1890 colleges and Tuskegee Institute almost one hundred years ago.

References

Carnegie Forum on Education and the Economy. *A Nation Prepared: Teachers for the Twenty-First Century: The Report of the Task Force on Teaching as a Profession, May 1986*. Washington, D.C.: The Forum, 1986.

Collison, M. N.-K. "More Young Black Men Choosing Not to Go to College." *Chronicle of Higher Education*. Issue 34, pg. A1, December 9, 1987.

Du Bois, W.E.B. *The Souls of Black Folks*. New York: Fawcett Publications, 1961, p. 79.

Magnuson, Ed. "7 Deadly Days." *Time: The Weekly News Magazine*, vol. 134, no. 3. 17 July 1989, pp. 30–60.

Mayberry, R.D. (Ed.). *Development of Research at Historically Black Land-Grant Institutions*. Jefferson City, Missouri: Association of Research Coordinators, 1976, p. 4.

Proctor, Samuel D. "Land-Grant Universities and the Black Presence." *Land-Grant Universities and Their Continuing Presence*. East Lansing, Michigan: Michigan State University Press, 1976, p. 193.

Rand, Ayn. *The Fountainhead*. New York: Signet Books, 1971, p. 679.

10

Education and Tomorrow's Work Force: A National Agenda

Clifton R. Wharton, Jr.

Today I want to address issues that go beyond agricultural economics, yet they are of urgent importance to you as scholars, as minorities, and as American citizens. Without being too dramatic, I can say that what I want to talk about is the sheer economic survival for the nation as a whole.

The United States stands on the verge of a revolution. And like most, this revolution is a mix of promise and peril.

Simply put, in the next decade, blacks and Hispanics are going to reshape the American work force. From now until the year 2000, new minority and immigrant entrants to the labor market will outnumber new white entrants by three to two. And by the turn of the century, or shortly afterward, one in every three U.S. residents will be nonwhite.

There is no mystery or conspiracy here. The reason is clear for anyone to see in the nation's vital statistics. For some time, the white birthrate has been falling to a point where it is now below the zero-population-growth level. The black birthrate is down too, but not by nearly as much. Because of this and immigration, the black and Hispanic fraction of the population is growing.

The nation's school systems reflect the transformation. Already our twenty-fivelargest city school systems have a majority of nonwhite students. In New York City, for example, the public schools are 79 percent nonwhite. In California, minorities are the majority in elementary schools statewide.

The trend is set for the foreseeable future. By the year 2000, what we see today in the schools will have become increasingly apparent in the adult work force as today's minority youth move into the nation's labor market in the years just ahead.

From now until the end of the twentieth century, an estimated 25 million people will be needed for the U.S. labor force. Native white males, who now constitute 47 percent of the labor force, will provide only 15 percent of all entrants to the labor force by the year 2000. Minorities and immigrants will provide about 60 percent.

Well, what's wrong with that? Doesn't it mean the country may finally be moving toward real equal employment opportunity?

On the surface, the answer would appear to be yes. The coming decades *can* be a time of tremendous opportunity for blacks and minorities. And everyone in this room can and should commit themselves to helping make sure it happens.

But serious obstacles and major pitfalls may block the way.

The problem isn't that minorities will be a growing presence in the work force. The problem, rather, is: Will they be able to do the kind of jobs the United States needs most?

The economy's greatest demand—and therefore the strongest job market—will be for highly educated, highly skilled workers. Yet because the next generation of American workers will include so many minorities, it will inevitably include a disproportionate number of poor people, high school dropouts, even functionally illiterate men and women.

Between now and 2000, nearly 1 out of 3 of the new work force entrants will come from single-parent homes. One out of 5 will have grown up in families below the poverty line. And according to the Children's Defense Fund, poor youths are almost 3 times more likely to drop out of high school than their peers who are not poor.

So when we look at today's poorest blacks and Hispanics, particularly at the so-called underclass in our major cities, we must ask ourselves some questions:

Do these children's early lives lay any groundwork at all for jobs that put an ever-higher premium on technical know-how?

How will these children develop the necessary skills, habits, and attitudes to take advantage of the changing labor market?

How can drug- and crime-ridden schools help disadvantaged children develop the skills and ambition to beat out the competition from abroad?

And if we can't somehow do a better job of preparing these children as the future workers of America, what will be our competitive prospects for the future?

Aging and Productivity

Complicating the picture even more is the aging of the population. In 1985, 28.5 million people were elderly (65 or over). By 2000, that number will increase to 34.9 million, and by 2010 it will be 39.2 million. Looking further out to 2030, when all the baby boomers will have reached age 65, the number will have soared to 64.6 million.

In 1950, 17 people were at work for every retired person. By 1992 that will have dropped to roughly 3 active workers for every retired person. And by 2015 or a little later, we could be looking at only 1.5 workers per retiree.

In the early years of the next millennium, we are anticipating one of the tightest labor markets in recent history. To sustain the economic growth the nation has experienced for decades—to address the glaring economic inequities that continue to mar American society—or simply to remain competitive in an expanding, global economy—we will need even greater productivity increases than the United States has seen over the last half-century.

The burden of achieving these increases will fall to a work force that will certainly be fewer in relation to those it supports. Unless we do something soon, tomorrow's work force will also be poorer, less skilled, and with a much higher fraction of young blacks and Hispanics from disadvantaged backgrounds. The result could be lower standards of living and less rewarding lives for an entire generation.

For over two years now I have served as cochairman of a task force of the Business-Higher Education Forum. I have been working with many other university leaders and corporate executives to develop a comprehensive picture of the coming impact of black and Hispanic Americans in the U.S. population and work force.

From our work, I am convinced we need a new national agenda for change. To work, the agenda must reflect experience and insights from virtually everyone—from public officials, private citizens, from government, business and non-profit institutions, and particularly from scholars and professionals such as yourselves.

With that in mind, I will touch on nine areas that I believe are central to the kind of national agenda we need if we are not to lose another generation of minority youngsters.

Area One: High School Graduation Rates

Since 1900 or so, the U.S. high school graduation rate climbed from 1 in 10 to 7 in 10. But as you know, not all groups do equally well.

In 1985 about half of all black 15- to 24-year-olds and about 40 percent of Hispanics had graduated—in each case, with women running slightly ahead of men. Again, that compares to around 72 percent of all white 15- to 24-year-olds.

Black graduation rates have recently been rising overall. But the dropout rate remains appallingly high in many areas, particularly inner-city school systems. Hispanic graduation seems to be dropping—from 36 percent of high school graduates in 1976 to 27 percent in 1985.

Elementary and high school preparation is the bedrock, the foundation for later achievement. Students from kindergarten to twelfth grade must learn the foundation skills—basic literacy, mathematics, and reasoning. Without such a foundation, there can be no progress in addressing the problems posed to our work force by the changing demographics.

Area Two: Teenage Full Employment

Teenage unemployment is a crippling problem for Blacks and Hispanics.

Especially in the cities, the shortage of after-school, weekend, and summer jobs has become central in sustaining the poverty cycle of the so-called underclass. Joblessness prevents young blacks and Hispanics from contributing to their family income and setting aside money for other purposes, such as future schooling.

At TIAA-CREF, where I am chairman, we have a number of programs to attack the problem. Our High School Cooperative Education Program offers part-time employment during the school year and full-time summer employment to high school students, most of them minorities. Our participation in the Summer Jobs For Youth Program provides high school and college students with summer employment. In addition, disadvantaged youths participating in the program have a chance to obtain full-time employment.

The point is that idle teenagers may come to see the underground economy, welfare dependency, and petty and serious crime as their only real choices. After-school and summer jobs help teenagers contribute to family support, build good work habits, and provide on-the-job skills training that may carry on into later life. And linking future job opportunities with staying in and graduating from high school is a promising way to reduce the dropout rate for blacks and Hispanics.

Areas Three and Four: College Attendance and Graduation Rates

From the 1960s into the early 1970s, blacks steadily closed the college attendance gap between them and the white majority.

Black attendance started to slide in 1977, when about half of all black high school grads were signing up for some form of post-secondary study. We hit a low point in 1982, when only 36 percent of recent black graduates headed for campuses. By 1985 black attendance was back up to 42 percent, but still below the 50 percent figure of the late seventies. As for Hispanics, their figures are well below white and black figures for comparable age groups.

Once in college, staying there can be even tougher. Blacks are only half as likely as whites to finish college. Up to half of black students leave college as freshmen or sophomores; the hemorrhaging continues afterward at a somewhat slower rate.

With the changes taking place, America's colleges, universities, and professional schools have a responsibility to strengthen their efforts to increase minority recruitment, retention, and graduation. This is where America's future professionals, leaders, and role models will be shaped. We must demand more cooperation between these institutions and K–12 educators to improve training and preparation of minority students.

When minority students do arrive, colleges must create an academic atmosphere that nurtures them and encourages them to succeed.*

Area Five: Graduate and Professional Studies

In 1987, blacks earned 904 research doctorates, 26.5 percent fewer than ten years before. Hispanics received only 709 Ph.D.s.

Although blacks were about 12 percent of the U.S. population in 1987, they received only about 3.5 percent of the doctorates granted to U.S. citizens in that year. Hispanic citizens, 8 percent of the U.S. population in 1987, received about 3 percent of the doctorates from our research universities.

Not only do minorities lag behind in graduate studies, but their areas of specialization run counter to workplace demand as well.

Of the 904 doctorates earned by blacks in 1987, about 413 are in education, 35 are in the physical sciences, 25 are in engineering, and 2 are in computer science. The shortage of blacks and Hispanics entering the key areas of the future work force will only serve to further restrict their entry into the top positions in business and industry, government, and civic affairs.

I would like to make one more point. I mentioned before that colleges and universities need to nurture minority students. Identifying and encouraging students capable of graduate work needs to be part of the nurturing process as early as possible. That means immediately upon college matriculation, if not before. The 1890 institutions are particularly well equipped to play a key role in this area.

Area Six: Faculty Representation

As part of the higher education initiatives I have touched on, we must not overlook the importance of faculty representation.

More than two-thirds of all black college students (and an even larger fraction of Hispanics) now attend predominately white institutions. In

---

*   The predominantly white campuses have much to learn in this area from traditionally black ones such as the 1890 institutions.

most cases, what this has meant up to now has too often been having a few minority instructors to conduct ethnic studies programs or to act as highly visible "role models." This is not a problem of the 1890 institutions, but those of you who have studied or taught at predominantly white campuses know what I mean.

This was never enough. Today it is intolerable.

Until blacks and Hispanics are a representative part of the broader academic community, is it not naive to expect more black and Hispanic success in undergraduate and graduate education? How otherwise can we hope for greater representation in the country's scientific, technical, professional, and managerial work force?

Area Seven: Private and Voluntary Organizations' Involvement

Because of governmental budgeting restrictions, we see today a constant battle going on to protect programs designed to increase minority advances and achievements. Broad new public initiatives meet ever stiffer resistance among taxpayers and voters.

The country's vast network of private and voluntary institutions must share the burden in ensuring continued progress on all fronts. Initiatives such as job training, scholarship and student assistance programs, talent searches, and internships need to be strengthened, not reduced. And many organizations that have such programs need to expand them.

Area Eight: Corporate Leadership

With few exceptions, our corporations have been less than successful in bringing blacks and Hispanics into executive and policy-making roles.

There are, of course, many firms with strong affirmative action records for entry-level and middle management. Even there, however, top black and Hispanic administrators are usually in short supply.

At my own company, TIAA-CREF, 46 percent of the staff is made up of minorities; nearly one-third is black. But our goals don't focus on numbers alone. We are trying to bring minority leaders into highly visible, influential roles. And we firmly believe if we as a company are to succeed in the future, we will have to succeed in this aspect of minority employment.

Today perhaps as never before, the long-range needs and interests of our nation's black and Hispanic minority are fundamentally at one with the needs of the society at large. Any company that eschews black and Hispanic leadership will be at increasing risk in a society where one-third of consumers and workers will soon be nonwhite, and where up to two-thirds of all new workers will be black or Hispanic.

Area Nine: Minority Leadership

Gradually—but certainly increasingly—minorities are occupying positions of influence and leadership in government, business, and academia. All of you here today are proof of that.

Leadership brings with it the added responsibility of setting an example. It is a responsibility none of us can ignore. You and your peers around the country must help motivate and inspire the many still trapped in poverty and hopelessness.

With leaders like yourselves, we increase daily our visible presence and effectiveness. We add to our resources, we spread the message. Ultimately, we add significantly to our prospects and power.

Conclusion

I said when I began that this was an issue of sheer economic survival for the nation as a whole.

For us in the black community, the situation translates broadly into two possible scenarios.

The first could be catastrophic. It would be disastrous not only for blacks, but for Hispanics and the country as a whole. In this scenario, the nation is caught unprepared by the coming revolution in the work force. Government and corporate efforts to respond remain isolated and inadequate—in effect, placing band-aids over gaping wounds. As the wounds go untreated, infection sets in, and the patient slowly deteriorates until there is no hope.

In real life, those wounds take the form of desperate family lives, crumbling school systems, soaring dropout rates, unemployment, crime, and drug addiction. The infections are endemic hopelessness and hate, despair and desolation. And for many, all hope truly is lost.

The United States must realize that, as disastrous as it sounds, this could be the terrifying reality in the years ahead.

But there is another scenario—one of promise, hope, and true opportunity.

It does not take a great deal of imagination to realize that if minorities will account for most of the growth in the work force, they will have a great opportunity to move ahead. For the first time, economic and demographic changes have created the absolute necessity to bring blacks, Hispanics, and other minorities into the mainstream of the U.S. work force. And in our second scenario, they are brought in along with the skills to rise successfully to the productivity challenges ahead.

What will take a great deal of imagination is developing the strategies to make the second scenario a reality. Indeed, I would argue that we need a full-scale blueprint for investing in the future—a comprehensive, national policy on minorities and the work force.

Once and for all, the country must awake to the realization that blacks, Hispanics, and other minorities are not now and certainly will not be in the future a burden to be lifted, but rather a great source for social and economic strength.

In an international economy that is increasingly interdependent, on a planet where the majority of the population is nonwhite, it is also an issue of simple realism. The question is not whether the U.S. *should* come to grips with the challenge. The question, rather, is whether we can do so in time to avert a precipitous decline of our national fortunes both at home and abroad.

To bring that realization about we need a new policy—a new agenda—a new plan. And it will have to be broader, more sweeping—a more courageous plan than any we have seen so far.

Quite simply, the full participation of blacks and minorities is vital to our success as a world leader and a prosperous, caring nation.

In the next quarter-century, minorities will be the most dynamic part of the U.S. work force. At the same time, the market for trained manpower will become increasingly competitive.

Because of these converging trends, the U.S. has both an urgent need and a once-in-a-lifetime opportunity.

For the first time, the dictates of national self-interest have become identical to those of national conscience. We *have* to bring blacks and

Hispanics fully into the work force. And because we have to, for the first time we may actually be *able* to.

It is not merely that a great deal is at stake.

What we honor in the American past is at stake.

What we cherish in the American present is at stake.

What we hope for in the American future is at stake.

For a society built on the ideals of freedom, equality, and full participation—*everything* is at stake. And the time to act is now.

PART IV

Policy Alternatives to Meet the Challenges of Institutional Design and Change

11

Designing Agricultural Institutions of Higher Education to Meet the Needs of the Twenty-First Century: Implications for Minorities

Melvin E. Walker, Jr.

This chapter focuses on two major areas: first, it briefly discusses the historical development and current roles of the 1890 Institutions, and second it identifies the challenges facing all of us in providing a well-trained cadre of professionals, especially minorities, who can fully participate in the agricultural and related sectors, both now and into the twenty-first century.

Historical Development of the 1890 Universities: Past and Present

At least three pieces of legislation are significant in the growth and development of the land-grant system as we know it today. The first is the Morrill Act of 1862, which authorized the establishment of a land-grant institution in each state to educate citizens in the fields of agriculture, home economics, the mechanic arts, and other useful professions. The second is the Hatch Act of 1887, which led to the creation of state agricultural experiment stations, and the third is the Smith Lever Act of 1914, which established the Cooperative Extension Service. In the South, blacks were not permitted to attend institutions established under the Morrill Act of 1862. This led to the passage of the Morrill Act of

1890 and the creation of 1890 Institutions in the southern states. Research and extension functions were added later under P.L. 89-106 and P. L. 95-113 (Sections 1444 and 1445), in 1967 and 1977 respectively.

During 1990, the 1890 Institutions are celebrating "A Century of Progress Through Teaching, Research and Extension." For nearly one hundred years, these institutions have played a significant role in the development of human resources, especially among blacks. Prior to 1965 they constituted the almost-exclusive source of professional expertise among blacks in the agricultural sciences. Service functions at most of these institutions were also targeted toward blacks.

With the passage of the Civil Rights Act of 1965, more blacks began to attend institutions of higher education created under the first Morrill Act. This trend has led to considerable concern and debate related to the continuing role and relevance of the 1890 universities. In spite of this debate, these institutions continue to exist and to provide for blacks and other minorities educational opportunities which are unparalleled by any other group of institutions.

While the scope of the mission of the 1890 Colleges and Universities has broadened over the years and appears, in some ways, to overlap that of the 1862 universities, there remains a major role to be played by these institutions.

Unfortunately, not all among us share this view. Some feel that the need and justification for the 1890 universities and other historically black colleges disappeared with the 1965 Civil Rights Act and the resulting integration of public colleges and universities. Others feel that since blacks and other minorities are now served by predominantly and historically white institutions, little justifies the continued existence of the 1890 institutions.

As long as there are people, problems, and limited resources, there will undoubtedly be a role for the 1890 universities and other historically black colleges, because these institutions have continued to achieve the goals for which they were established—to provide quality educational opportunities for all, particularly minorities and other disadvantaged groups.

The 1890 institutions and other historically black colleges and universities have provided that quality education to many thousands of black Americans, many of whom may otherwise have been denied opportunities for higher education. These institutions have served as a bridge between high school and the graduate schools of 1862 and other major institutions. A vast majority of all blacks with advanced degrees in agriculture, for example, are products of undergraduate programs at 1890 institutions. With blacks and other minorities projected to constitute a major share of the labor force by the turn of the century, it is clear that the 1890 universities and other historically black institutions can and must continue to play a significant role in providing educational opportunities. The accomplishments of the 1890 universities and other historically black institutions are nothing less than phenomenal, especially when one considers that these accomplishments were made in spite of the sometimes inadequate support received.

While the methods of and approaches to achieving the mission may differ in the future, the role of the 1890 universities will remain unchanged—to provide opportunity and the development of human capital to meet the needs of a changing society. We will continue to evaluate our programs and to enhance and develop them to meet these needs as we have for more than one hundred years. We will also continue to work to assure that our programs complement rather than duplicate those offered at the 1862 schools.

The Challenge: Assuring the Supply of Well-trained Minority Professionals

Yet, the real issue is deeper than the survival of the 1890 Institutions and the role they will play in higher education in the future. More important, instead, is the assurance of minority participation in the land-grant system, whether at 1890, 1862, or other institutions. It won't matter much whether 1890 institutions survive if minorities are not ready to accept the challenge to assume roles of importance and leadership. While opportunities in agriculture are virtually limitless for minorities, what is needed are programs designed to prepare minorities for the opportunities which now exist and for those expected to exist in the twenty-first century. This initiative will require a commitment from all—the private sector, the 1890 Colleges and Universities, the 1862 Universities, U.S. Department of Agriculture (USDA), and other related agencies. It will require a level of cooperation never before witnessed.

To achieve this, several members of the 1890 community have conceptualized a plan which offers the potential for increasing the

numbers of minorities in agriculture and related sciences, especially at
the advanced degree level. This program involves several requirements
which tend to influence the success of any program involving changing
the attitudes and behavior of human subjects. These requirements are
(1) early intervention, (2) an adequate supply of resources, and (3)
inordinate levels of commitment and cooperation.

First, we must begin with early forms of intervention. Because of
historical experiences and negative views of agriculture held by most
blacks, early intervention programs are needed to reach young blacks
early to help shape their attitudes and values well in advance of the senior
year of high school. We must reach them in the formative years if
success is to be achieved. The USDA Minority Research Appren-
ticeship Program is an excellent example of the effectiveness of early
intervention programs. This program has been in effect since 1979 and
involves bringing junior and senior high school students to land-grant
campuses and federal agencies and involving them in the research
process. Students are introduced to agriculture and the scientific method
of inquiry. This program has provided opportunity and encouragement
to hundreds of minority students. Almost 100 percent of the participants
have gone on to college and many of them have majored in agriculture
and/or related sciences. Some have obtained advanced degrees. This
program is probably the most successful we have had in this area.

The next requirement involves resources—more specifically, money.
If minorities are going to be attracted to agriculture and related sciences,
we must invest dollars for scholarships, assistantships, internships, and
the like. Minorities with good academic records are sought with "big
bucks" by many colleges and universities boasting the glamorous side
of life. We must offer good financial packages in order to be competitive
with these institutions.

We must not rely solely on the federal government to provide resources for the development of minority talent. Institutions committed to
this effort must "dig deep" to find resources to support it. Public and
private agencies at all levels must be involved and must contribute as
the need dictates.

Finally, we must bring together extension, research, and teaching on
1890 campuses to support these efforts at both the undergraduate and
graduate levels. Student involvement must become a major component
of our programs. These three units garner a significant pool of resources

that can and must be better utilized in our effort to meet the challenge of minority resource development.

Having enumerated the major factors believed to influence the success of this program, allow me to now present the gist of the proposed program and indicate what can be done to support its implementation. The success of the program depends significantly upon the cooperation and commitment of leaders in elementary and high schools, land-grant institutions, and both public and private agencies. What is needed is a package that we can take to an eighth grader and say, "If you will follow a prescribed course of study during your four years of high school and complete your course-work with a C+ or better average, we will guarantee you a place in college at a participating 1890 Institution." Further, "If you successfully complete the prescribed course of study in college with a B average or better, we will guarantee your acceptance at a participating 1890 or 1862 Institution to pursue graduate study." These guarantees will be supported by financial and other contributions from private and public agencies, educational institutions, and private businesses.

Implementation of the plan will include a number of activities with roles for both 1890 and 1862 Institutions. The goal is to aid minority students in making the transition from a rural, family-oriented environment to that found on major 1862 campuses. The program will be initiated by the 1890 institutions who will have identified potential students during or at completion of the eighth grade. These students will be brought to 1890 campuses during the summer where they will be introduced to agriculture, related sciences, and college life. Working through high school counselors and advisors, courses of study will be developed for grades 9 through 12. Then, students will return to campus at least once per quarter or semester to spend a few hours with college officials, faculty, and students. They will also return to campus for each of the next four summers for instruction in science, mathematics, chemistry, physics, communications, and agriculture. Additionally, they will receive instruction in research methods.

Upon graduation from high school, students will enroll in an 1890 college with a preplanned course of study leading to the bachelor's degree. Students will immediately select one or more institutions from among participating 1862 Universities that they wish to consider for graduate study. With consideration given to tactical arrangements, students will also be required to enroll in courses for one quarter or semester during each of the junior and senior years and each summer at the chosen 1862 Institution. In addition to an on-site advisor at the 1862 Institution, these students will have visiting advisors assigned from the 1890 Institutions. Upon completion of the bachelor's degree, eligible students will enroll for graduate study at an 1862 or 1890 Institution.

This program is designed to provide individual attention and support throughout the educational process. We believe that this is an important element in attracting and retaining minority students. What is needed to make this program work are individuals and institutions that are willing to make commitments. If each terminal, degree-granting 1862 Institution would commit to at least two students annually in any area, we can increase the supply of black professionals in agriculture by at least 600 by the year 2000. Together, we can make a difference.

In closing, a quote from James T. Bonnen "The Institutional Structure Associated with Agricultural Science: What Have We Learned?" may be appropriate.

> Man, not science, transformed U.S. agriculture. Men and women, acting through the institutions that they created, developed scientific knowledge, changed human values and aspirations, modified old institutions and built new ones as they saw the need, and step by step transformed the productivity of agriculture and the welfare of U.S. farmers and consumers.

I contend that as people made the difference in transforming U.S. agriculture, they will also make the difference in developing minority talent for tomorrow's agriculture and the continued success of a nation.

References

Bonnen, James T. "The Institutional Structure Associated with Agricultural Science: What Have We Learned?" In *Agricultural Science Policy in Transition*, edited by James Rhodes. Bethesda, Md.: Agricultural Research Institute, 1986, pp. 37–68.

12

Keeping the Land-Grant Tradition: The Future Roles of the 1890 Land-Grant Institutions

James T. Bonnen

Throughout the 1980s, black enrollments have been declining at all U.S. colleges and universities while Asian and Hispanic enrollments have risen. Black enrollments at black institutions have begun to rise again since 1987 (Magner, 1988). In recent years, some 1890 universities have also experienced an increasing proportion of white enrollment, especially those institutions that play regional four-year and local community college roles providing low-cost, accessible education for those who are not wealthy and whose educational options are circumscribed. In assessing the future role of the 1890 institutions one must understand the universal discrimination in funding that they have experienced (Seals, 1988). These institutions have long been starved for resources and continue to be so. The 1890 institutions are very diverse and are situated in quite different environments. Thus, future roles are likely to differ substantially from one institution to another.

In my judgement, the single most important future role of the 1890 institutions is carrying on the land-grant tradition. The land-grant idea is slowly dying as today's 1862 land-grant institutions attempt to emulate American Association of Universities (AAU) institutions. The consequence is that they are becoming more and more expensive and elitist in outlook and less responsive to the problems of people in their state and

129

local communities. The only real potential for carrying the land-grant idea into the twenty-first century lies with the 1890 universities. This is where the land-grant idea is still alive and vital.

You have only to visit an 1890 campus to see this. The 1890 universities still believe. Today the 1862 institutions either do not believe or no longer understand the land-grant idea. A central feature of the land-grant idea was providing access to higher education for capable young people of limited means and inadequate preparation. Besides blacks in general, the targets for the 1890 institutions in the future are those adults, especially single parents in need of education who are trying to escape poverty and to provide for their families. The 1890 universities, if located near major population centers and not faced with direct community college and four-year college competition, can play this role. Included in this are low income, disadvantaged whites who are in just as great a need of education (Swarns, 1988; Lock, 1988). The central problem of higher education for the disadvantaged is not so much recruitment as it is retention. The black and Hispanic dropout rate is far too high, especially in the predominantly white private and public institutions. One key to successful retention appears to lie in teaching such students cooperative study habits, i.e., learning to work together in groups. The institution should be responsible for developing support systems and encouraging students to develop habits of working together in educating each other as well as going to class and studying (Richardson, 1989).

Only 16 percent of all black college students were enrolled in the 104 traditional black institutions in 1982–1983, while 44 percent of full-time black faculty taught at traditional black institutions. Many of the remaining 56 percent of black faculty teach in highly urban institutions which, while not intended so, today have predominantly black or minority enrollments (Orlans, 1988).

In my judgement, the U.S. is both schizophrenic and hypocritical in its attitudes toward the 104 traditional black institutions of higher education. It is schizophrenic in the sense that it sends conflicting signals for the policy direction and role of these institutions. It is hypocritical in that it knowingly attempts at one in the same time to impose integration rules while discriminating grossly in the funding of 1890 universities and other public black institutions. The consequence is that many of these institutions are in trouble: (1) financially, (2) in their ability to attract good students, including good black students, and (3) in their ability to attract and hold the best black faculty. The elite (mostly private) black institutions are, in general doing better. They attract middle and upper class black enrollment and the subsequent alumni financial support that helps create a more stable institutional foundation.

The public institutions are an entirely different matter. Public policy has directed that institutions of higher learning staff their faculties with minorities at least in proportion to their representation in the Ph.D. universe from which a particular field draws. The reality, of course, is that the majority of black faculty are concentrated in predominantly black institutions, whether traditional black institutions or institutions that are perforce highly black in both student body and faculty. Harold Orlans argues that "higher education cannot successfully pursue policies of both dispersing and concentrating minority and female faculty members" (ibid.).

In many professions, especially law, medicine, nursing, library science, and teaching, the vast majority of today's black professionals received their training from predominately black institutions such as Howard, Texas Southern, Southern of Louisiana, Meharry, Atlanta, and others. For the foreseeable future this will continue to be so. The efforts to merge or close black professional schools in some states, such as the proposed merger of the Louisiana State University law school with that of Southern University, are destructive (and hypocritical) as long as stringent admission standards and failure to provide equal support for the K-12 and college education of blacks (and others) at predominately black public institutions persists (Cage, 1989). The best that can be said of such action is that it is premature or misinformed. It is certainly not in the interest of a society that desires blacks to achieve the same educational levels as the rest of society.

As President Wharton has just outlined for us, labor force projections to the year 2000 show that a majority of the new entrants to the labor force will be minorities—primarily blacks, Hispanics, and Asians. The education, health and other human capabilities of the U.S. labor force is at hazard if minority education, health, etc. is not improved. This is not, as President Wharton indicates, a black or minority problem but a society-wide threat to U.S. productivity and international competitiveness. We do not have time to wait for discrimination to disappear. We must invest now in the education of black, Hispanic and other minority and poor children, and young adults wherever they are and wherever they choose to attend school.

To succeed in achieving any goal, an institution must reflect the values inherent in such goals. Today the only institutions that still clearly reflect the land-grant ideal and goals are the 1890 universities and some community colleges and regional four-year colleges. In the November 9, 1988 issue of the *Wall Street Journal*, a feature column discussed the dilemma and difficulties of the 1890 traditional black institutions of higher education (Swarns, 1988). Subsequently on December 12, 1988, the following letter to the editor appeared:

It was my good fortune to graduate from Lincoln University in Missouri, the original all-black college you highlighted in your November 9, page 1 article "Black Colleges Turn Increasingly White in a Fight to Survive." I am white and was in the minority at Lincoln, from which I graduated in 1965. I won an academic scholarship, awarded me by the black administration—not because I was black or white, but because of need. Like many of the black students who came before, LU was my only opportunity to pursue higher education and it was, and is, higher education.

Many of my black professors, had they been white, would have commanded far higher salaries elsewhere. My training by them makes it possible for me today to run my own million-dollar business, some of the proceeds of which are annually awarded to LU students as scholarships.

Lincoln, and black colleges across the country, began because of discrimination. It is sad that the opening of educational opportunities for blacks in all schools weakens the appeal of these pioneering black schools that did so much—with so little—for so long. But I submit that schools like Lincoln are growing with the times providing invaluable roles, both in education and race relations. I'm proud to be an LU graduate, and have found my "black" degree has prepared me well for life, business and subsequent education.

Like the many black students who came before us, we white newcomers knew such an educational opportunity would not come our way again. We, in Lincoln, made the most of the situation. There are thousands of your readers who owe much to schools like Lincoln, and they are black, and they are white. I'd challenge those who've benefitted so much from such schools to come through now, when your school and its current students, needs help. It's called a contribution to your school's scholarship or general fund. What if your school had not been there when you needed it?

Gene Lock, President
Lock Agency, Inc.
Sacramento, California

References

Cage, Mary Crystal. "Court Orders Louisiana To Alter College Governance, Abolish Southern University Board." *Chronicle of Higher Education*, 26 July 1989, pp. 19, 20.

Lock, Gene. Letter to the Editor. *Wall Street Journal*, 12 December 1988, p. A-13.

Magner, Denise K. and Jean Evangelauf. "Enrollment Has Risen At Many Black Colleges This Fall." *Chronicle of Higher Education*, 26 October 1988, pp. A1, 41, 42.

Orlans, Harold. "National Faculty Hiring Goals Flout Demands Of Many Women and Members Of Minority Groups." *Chronicle of Higher Education*, 17 February 1988, pp. B1, 2.

Richardson, Richard C. "If Minority Students Are To Succeed In Higher Education, Every Rung Of The Educational Ladder Must Be In Place." *Chronicle of Higher Education*, 11 January 1989, p. A48.

Seals, R. Grant. "Pursuit Of Quality Education: The Land-Grant Exclusion Principle." *The Forty-Fifth Annual Professional Agricultural Workers Conference: 1987 Proceedings*, Tuskegee, Alabama: Tuskegee University, 1988, pp. 67–75.

Swarns, Rachel. "Black Colleges Turn Increasingly White In A Fight To Survive." *Wall Street Journal*, 9 November 1988, pp. 1, 6.

13

Reforming Land-Grant Institutions to Educate Young People for Professional Careers in Agriculture

Mason C. Carter

I want to address in my opening remarks two topics of concern in considering alternative institutional design for the land-grant system in the South. First, I want to comment on the subject of recruiting and educating people for professional careers in agriculture regardless of the type of institution (1862, 1890, or non-land-grant). Then I will address the future roles as I see them for the 1890 and 1862 institutions.

Undergraduate enrollment in colleges of agriculture has consistently and almost universally declined over the past decade. If we consider only U.S. citizens and traditional agricultural disciplines, graduate enrollment has also declined sharply. As a result, we have widespread forecasting of shortages of scientists, engineers, and managers for our food and agriculture agencies and businesses.

This trend is not a problem for the general public. Business and industry will find the people they need—if not in our colleges of agriculture, then from colleges of business, arts and science, etc. However, declining enrollments are a major problem for colleges of agriculture. Why have enrollments declined at a time when job openings and career opportunities are abundant?

Well, for one thing, the career opportunities are not those typically perceived by high school students as agricultural careers. The oppor-

tunities are in agribusiness: marketing, not of farm products, but marketing of products and services to the farmer, or processing and marketing
of food, clothing or other manufactured products derived from agriculture; management and finance, not of production farming, but of
manufacturing, retailing, international trade; research and development,
not just for farm productivity, but for new products and services, for
human nutrition and health, for environmental enhancement, recreation,
leisure and the quality of life. Graduates in traditional disciplines such
as agronomy, agricultural economics, pest management, are more likely
to work as salesmen or consultants than as producers or practitioners.

Nearly one-third of the U.S. gross national product is generated by
food-related businesses. The milling and processing of grains and
vegetables, the processing of meat, poultry and seafood, the operations
of grocery and eating establishments—these provide numerous career
opportunities for graduates of colleges of agriculture. And what about
environmental management? Whether it's plantscaping an office building or landscaping a city park or national forest, colleges of agriculture
have the capacity to prepare graduates for such careers. College students
are looking for interesting and rewarding careers. If we convince them
and their parents that a major in the college of agriculture offers such
career opportunities, they will enroll.

Recruiting teams must consist of appropriate role models. High
school students want to talk to college students. Parents want to talk to
faculty and deans. There should be male and female, majority and
minority representation. And, last, but by no means least, employers.
Employers have an important role to play in helping recruit students into
agriculture and in advising students and faculty on necessary education
and personal skills required for career success.

To be fully effective, a career information campaign must be accom-
panied by a program of scholarships or other financial assistance. You
cannot greatly influence students to study agriculture with scholarships
unless they are already interested in the field. However, you can enable
many students interested in agriculture to attend an 1862 or 1890
institution who might otherwise not attend college or attend another
institution.

Enrollment trends can be reversed. They have been at Louisiana State
University and elsewhere. An example of a successful program is here
at Southern University's College of Agriculture and Home Economics.

Dean Bobby Phills' BAYOU (Beginning Agricultural Opportunity Unit) program has significantly increased the number of capable students enrolled in his college.

Retention is the third important factor in enrollment management, with both curricular and non-curricular dimensions. Non-curricular aspects—counseling, monitoring, personal attention—are not unique to agriculture. The curricular aspect is unique to agriculture and is, perhaps, the most significant factor influencing the future of both undergraduate and graduate programs in colleges of agriculture at both 1862 and 1890 institutions.

Most faculty in colleges of agriculture at 1862 and 1890 institutions hold joint appointments between instruction and agricultural experiment stations (AES) and/or cooperative extension services (CES). Typically, 75 to 80 percent of faculty time is assigned to experiment station and/or extension functions. By design and necessity, the programs and faculty interest of the AES and CES are concentrated in agricultural production, producers, and primary processors. But that is not where most career opportunities for our graduates lie. Our research and extension is focused primarily on enhancing the quantity, quality, and profitability of farming. The same faculty conducting these research and extension programs for farmers are teaching our undergraduate and graduate courses. Much talk is given to changing the "image" or the "perception" of agriculture and agricultural curricula. *For the most part, the image is correct!!!* In many of our courses, we are still teaching people how to farm. We must change the approach to most of our courses and curricula. To do that means we must change the focus and direction of the faculty, their research, and their extension efforts. This transformation will be a far more difficult task than recruitment, for it will require a fundamental change in objectives and orientation of faculty and their programs. Few institutions can afford to maintain separate instructional faculties. Fewer still can afford to hire new faculty for the purpose of reorienting courses and curricula. It is an interesting challenge.

Colleges of agriculture are developing the techniques for recruitment of adequate numbers of capable students. Freshman enrollment is up on a number of campuses. But retention and long-term success will require that we develop new courses and curricula better-suited to prepare graduates for careers in the nonfarming sector of the agro-industrial complex of the world.

Now for some comments on the future of 1890 institutions in particular.

Whenever I think of this subject I am reminded of the comments of an elderly black man that I heard in 1959 in Macon, Georgia. School integration was a very new topic at that time, and a committee of the Georgia legislature was holding hearings to determine how Georgia citizens, especially black citizens felt about the idea. "Separate-but-equal" public schools was the policy preferred by most of the white population. At one of the public hearings, an elderly black man was asked his opinion of the separate-but-equal concept. His reply, as best as I can recall, was:

> "It may be all right, but so far I've seen a whole lot of emphasis on separate, but not much on equal."

The 1890 institutions were founded on the concept of "separate-but-equal." Over the past century we have certainly accomplished the separate part. The 1890 institutions and the 1862 institutions in the same states are probably the most racially segregated institutions in all of higher education.

Equal they are not; at least not in size, scope and budgets. Would making them equal solve the undesirable racial imbalances? This idea has not been very successful in elementary and secondary education. Is there reason to believe it can succeed in higher education? Would it be in the best interest of our citizens to have two completely equal, but segregated, land-grant institutions in a state? Alternatively, does it make sense to develop two fully integrated but essentially duplicate land-grant institutions in a state? The latter makes more sense than the former. In states with a sufficiently large tax base and agriculture base, two or more land-grant institutions may be justified. Especially, if they are geographically separated so as to service different regions of the state. California and Texas already have multiple institutions on the land-grant model.

But in Arkansas and Mississippi the tax base is hardly sufficient to support one competitive land-grant institution. Here in Louisiana the 1862 and 1890 institutions are less than ten miles apart. Another approach would appear more feasible.

I believe agriculture programs should move toward a system of merger and coordination: merger into a single AES and CES, and coordination of undergraduate and graduate education. AES and CES should be planned and managed statewide under a single system. The University of California System is an example. Faculty qualifications, recruitment, evaluation, promotion, and compensation would be the same at all locations.

The college of agriculture at the 1862 campus would become quite selective in freshman admissions. Because of their strong developmental programs, 1890 institutions might choose to be less selective. Students who were not prepared for admission to the 1862 school as a freshman could attend the 1890 or another institution until completing the equivalent of the sophomore year. *All students successfully completing the junior division program at a public institution would be admitted to the senior college at the 1862 or 1890 institution.*

1890 institutions would offer baccalaureate programs in selected areas of agriculture, either unique to that campus or duplicative of programs on the 1862 campus. *However, all four-year programs offered on the 1890 campus would have the same entrance requirements to the senior college (Junior year) as four-year programs on the 1862 campus. Course contents and examinations would be closely coordinated for duplicate or similar programs.*

Graduate programs would be concentrated on the 1862 campus, but there would be selected Ph.D. programs also available at the 1890 campus. However, the graduate faculties would be merged with a single set of criteria and the same selection procedures.

The alternative is to continue to go our separate ways—two groups of institutions, racially segregated, but almost identically organized and directed. One survives only because the other fails to do its job efficiently and thoroughly. I do not believe it is in the best interest of future generations to perpetuate the current system.

14

Reforming Agricultural Science Professions to Enhance the Status and Opportunities for Black Professionals: Policy Implications for Agricultural Economists

Carlton G. Davis

Meaningful discussion of the policy issues stemming from the study *Opportunities and Status of Blacks in Agricultural Economics* (Allen, Davis, Evans, et al., 1985) takes place within the context of the environment in which the profession operates. To do otherwise would be to flagrantly and unwisely disregard the interactive impacts of environmental changes on the labor market for agricultural economists in general, and black agricultural economists in particular. That there are major environmental changes occurring in the profession is a well-recognized fact. Polopolus and Harl cogently reviewed some of the important changes in their recent Agricultural Economics Association (AAEA) presidential addresses. Harl argues that "agricultural economics may be moving into the most important, and possibly the most turbulent period in the history of the profession" (Harl, 1983:845).

One area of concern that is directly relevant to black agricultural economists is the question whether graduate and undergraduate agricultural economics programs (the supply side) are adjusting rapidly enough, and with sufficient breadth, to enable the important agricultural economics functions (the demand side) to be carried out (Harl, 1983). To the extent that environmental changes impacting the profession are likely to affect the status and opportunities of black agricultural economists, it is important to review some of the important changes and draw policy inferences for the group. In this regard, this paper will first re-review important environmental changes within the agricultural economics profession. Second, it will attempt to relate some of these changes to policy issues relevant to black agricultural economists, given the findings of the Committee on Opportunities and Status of Blacks in Agricultural Economics (COSBAE). The discussion of environmental changes will draw heavily on a recent study by Blank (1985) focusing on agricultural economics programs in the United States and Canada over the 1975–1984 period. The particular aspects of environmental changes evaluated were (1) student enrollment, (2) student composition, and (3) academic program areas. The characteristics of these three components are discussed below.

Agricultural Economics Program Environment

Enrollment Trends 1975–1984

Over the 1975–1984 period, undergraduate enrollment in U.S. agricultural economics programs increased significantly, while graduate enrollment remained fairly constant. Disaggregation of enrollment figures for five U.S. geographical regions (West, Central, North Central, South, and Northeast) and Canada reveal important regional variations. All five regions and Canada registered a 61 percent increase in undergraduate agricultural economics enrollment. The U.S. region with the lowest rate of undergraduate increase (27 percent) for the period was the South. It was noted that this undergraduate enrollment trend in the South was a reversal of the trend from the 1970–1975 period, as reported in a study by Beck, et al. (1977). According to the earlier 1970–1975 data, the South registered the fastest rate of undergraduate agricultural economics enrollment.

At the graduate level, one-half of the regions experienced an increase in average year-to-year enrollment, while one-half experienced a decline. These counter movements resulted in no change in graduate enrollment over the period. One interesting trend was the direction of graduate and undergraduate enrollment in the Northeast and South. Specifically, the Northeast, which experienced the highest rate of growth

(86 percent) in undergraduate enrollment, concurrently experienced the highest rate of decline (32 percent) in graduate enrollment over the period. Also, the South, which experienced the lowest rate of growth (27 percent) in undergraduate enrollment, concurrently experienced the highest rate of growth (92 percent) in graduate enrollment over the period.

These observed trends in aggregate graduate and undergraduate agricultural economics enrollment raise a number of perplexing questions for the agricultural economics profession. Intuitively, one would have expected that graduate agricultural economics enrollment would have increased over the 1975–1984 period with an increased aggregate pool of undergraduate majors to draw upon. This, however, did not appear to have occurred. A number of possible explanations have been offered, including: (1) increasing noncompetitiveness of agricultural economics programs with business schools for M.S. and Ph.D. students seeking to meet corporate demand for training in agribusiness management; (2) conscious policies of graduate agricultural economics programs to maintain a desired student/faculty ratio in the face of declining budget allocations; (3) some reallocation of program resources away from graduate training towards undergraduate training, in the face of increasing undergraduate enrollment; and (4) the high opportunity cost of pursuing graduate training in agricultural economics in light of declining real salaries for agricultural economists.

Student Composition and Program Area Trends 1975–1984

The significant changes observed in the last two decades in the composition of agricultural economics students continued over the 1975–1984 period. Some of the major changes are: (1) an increasing proportion of agricultural economics students with nonfarm background; (2) an increasing proportion of female students entering agricultural economics programs, particularly at the graduate level; (3) an increasing proportion of graduate students with nonagricultural economics majors at the undergraduate level; and (4) an increasing proportion of graduate-level foreign students. Concurrent with the changing composition of the student population, there have been major programmatic changes in agricultural economics. Both student composition changes and program area changes are important dimensions of the supply and demand components of the future agricultural economics labor market. These changes undoubtedly will impact the status and opportunities for blacks in the agricultural economics profession.

Major differences appear to exist in both the composition and the growth rates of agricultural economics options at the undergraduate and graduate levels. Most graduate agricultural economics programs consist primarily of traditional subject matter options, such as farm management/production economics, agricultural marketing, price and income analysis, international trade and development, and agribusiness. In contrast, undergraduate programs often tend to have a wide variety of subject matter options in addition to the more traditional options.

Some interesting growth variations are occurring, however, between undergraduate and graduate program areas. Departments were asked to identify the anticipated growth areas over the next decade (1984–1994), and these were compared with projected growth areas for the previous decade. Specifically, the anticipated high growth areas for undergraduate options after 1975 were agribusiness, farm management/production economics, natural resources, and rural development. Data indicate that the agribusiness undergraduate option is still expected to be the high growth area in the next decade. However, farm management/production economics, natural resources, and rural development are projected to experience significant declines. It is suggested that the anticipated growth in the post-1975 period for these areas might have been realized by 1984. As the demand declined for these areas, there has been an accompanying shift away from these options.

There are a number of interesting regional variations in the anticipated undergraduate growth areas over the next decade. All U.S. regions anticipated that the undergraduate agribusiness area will be the first or second growth area in the next decade. Of particular interest is the fact that all of the non-Land-Grant agricultural economic programs (13 percent of the total respondents) listed agribusiness as the greatest anticipated growth area for undergraduate enrollment. Also, at the undergraduate level, 50 percent of Northeastern agricultural economics programs anticipated no growth in their farm management/production economic option. In contrast 60 percent of Southern programs listed this option first or second in anticipated growth over the next decade. Also, of particular interest, the South was the only region to project significant growth in their undergraduate marketing option in the years to come.

In terms of graduate level programs, there was less concentration of projected growth areas than those exhibited at the undergraduate level. Specifically, as was the case at the undergraduate level, a strong growth potential was projected for the agribusiness option at the graduate level. However, unlike the undergraduate options, at the graduate level the traditional agricultural economics areas received the largest number of "first" and "second" place growth area rankings for the next decade. Specifically, the farm management/production economics, international trade/development, and quantitative methods areas all received significantly higher growth potential ranking at the graduate level. It is postulated that the projected differences in growth areas at the under-graduate and graduate levels are reflections of differences in the projected demand for types of human capital stocks during the next decade.

Policy Implications for Black Agricultural Economists

Agricultural economics program environment will undoubtedly impact the current and future labor market situations for black agricultural economists. Since the basic components of the profession's labor market are its supply and demand configuration, these two dimensions will be discussed, relative to policy issues stemming from COSBAE's study.

Supply Dimensions

The aggregate supply function for black agricultural economists would embody (1) practicing black agricultural economists with different levels of academic qualifications, (2) black undergraduate agricultural economics students, and (3) black graduate agricultural economics students. This supply function can be described, among other things, as exhibiting the following general characteristics: (1) underrepresentation of blacks in the agricultural economics profession, (2) a preponderance of black agricultural economists at the B.S. and M.S. degree levels, (3) concentration of black Ph.D.s at predominantly black educational institutions, (4) persistently rigid in the outward direction over time, and

(5) shows limited potential for significant reduction in its outward rigidity in the near future.

A number of interesting policy issues revolve around the relationship of programmatic environmental changes to these supply characteristics. At the undergraduate level it is obvious that the number of black undergraduate agricultural economists majors was not an integral part of the increased undergraduate agricultural economics enrolled observed over the 1974–1984 period. The study on black agricultural economists reported that in 1983, black undergraduate majors accounted for 150 of 5,000 (3 percent) of the undergraduate agricultural economics majors at 46 academic institutions. Most of these black undergraduates were enrolled at predominantly black institutions, which are located primarily in the South. As indicated earlier, the South experienced the slowest rate of undergraduate agricultural economics enrollment over the 1975–1984 period, which was a reversal of the 1970–1975 trend. Given these trends, it would seem reasonable to assume that there would be some concomitant negative effects on the level of black undergraduate agricultural economics enrollment over the 1975–1984 period, given their concentration in the South. This appears to have been the case. A U.S. Department of Education study indicated a 1.6 percent decline in the number of B.S. agricultural economics degrees awarded to blacks over the 1976–1981 period.

What are the major factors associated with declining black undergraduate agricultural economics enrollment in the face of significant increase in aggregate undergraduate agricultural economics enrollment? A number of possible explanations may be offered. First, the retrenchment of agriculture-related programs, including agricultural economics, at many 1890 institutions in the 1970s might have resulted in a dramatic decline in aggregate black undergraduate agricultural economics enrollment, since these institutions produce the bulk of such students. Many such institutions were mandated under court-ordered Equal Employment Opportunity and Affirmative Action decrees to expand the range of subject matter offerings to attain parity with 1862 institutions, and to attract a wider cross section of students. Under such decrees, many of these institutions consolidated their agricultural programs and established a wider variety of technical and business-related options. These changes might have resulted in shifts away from agricultural economics areas. Second, many of the potential black undergraduate agricultural economics majors at 1890 institutions might have elected to attend predominantly white institutions and major in higher demand areas other than agricultural economics. This second factor might have been significant, since over the period many predominantly white institutions were also mandated to increase their black student enrollment. Many were able to attract black undergraduate students through lucrative financial aid and scholarship packages.

At the graduate level, black graduate enrollment represents a small proportion of total graduate agricultural economics enrollment. The 1983 survey data from 46 graduate agricultural economics programs indicate that at the M.S. level there were 36 blacks in an enrollment of 1,000 student (3.6 percent). At the Ph.D. level, there were only 15 blacks in an enrollment of 800 students (1.9 percent). These enrollment figures indicate a relatively small pool and a stagnant rate of growth in the supply of graduate level black agricultural economists. It also indicates that very little potential exists for future increase in the supply of practicing black agricultural economists, particularly at the Ph.D. level. This is cause for serious concern, since the trend within the agricultural economics profession is one of a sustained movement towards a high proportion of Ph.D. degree holders. Furthermore, the data indicate that black graduate students have not been a significant part of the changing enrollment composition observed over the 1975–1984 period. Blacks have not been a significant factor in the changing gender composition of graduate agricultural economics programs. Of particular interest is the fact that the proportion of black female graduate students in agricultural economics programs is minimal, particularly at the Ph.D. level. Since the pool of practicing black female agricultural economists is already minimal, it is clear that there is limited potential for augmenting this pool in the near future from the ranks of graduate students.

What are the factors associated with the persistently low enrollment of blacks in agricultural economics programs? The major factors would include, among other things, perception of career opportunities, barriers to entry and career advancement, and opportunity cost of time. What are the specific objectives of black agricultural economists? Data indicate striking similarity between black and nonblack graduate degree candidates with respect to career objectives. University teaching and research activities, and research activities in government agencies are the most frequently cited career goals for blacks with graduate agricultural economics training, regardless of undergraduate educational background.

In general, black agricultural economists felt that they have been able to pursue their career objectives. There is strong indication, however, that blacks have not been able to pursue the full range of career objectives within the limits of the wider professional labor market. The high concentration of black Ph.D. level agricultural economists at predominantly black academic institutions strongly suggests that blacks with Ph.D. level training are forced through institutionalized segmented academic labor markets to pursue their career objectives at predominantly black institutions. This amounts to *de facto* job reserving among academic institutions, whereby black professionals are restricted to institutions serving black clients. This proposition is further supported by the fact that the few black Ph.D. agricultural economists who were employed at predominantly white educational institutions were employed in the South, the region with the greatest concentration of blacks. As such, their employment might also be directly related to their employers' desire to utilize their training in service to black clients.

It could be argued, however, that the supply orientation of black Ph.D. agricultural economists is simply a reflection of major differences in the stocks of human capital that they possess, *vis-à-vis* nonblack Ph.D.s. This does not appear to be the case, however, since black Ph.D.s were equally likely as nonblack Ph.D.s to specialize in the traditionally popular areas of farm management/production economics, marketing, international trade and development. In short, black Ph.D.s appear to have the specialized training needed to conduct research in high priority agricultural economic areas. As such, other factors must be influencing the size of the academic labor market with respect to the utilization of high levels black human capital stocks. To the extent that institutional factors are in part responsible for the narrowness of the labor market for black Ph.D.s, these factors would act as long-term disincentive to the acquisition of improved human capital. Data indicate that blacks were somewhat less optimistic than nonblacks regarding career opportunities. Practicing black Ph.D.s were significantly less optimistic regarding career opportunities.

Entry level and career advancement barriers would reinforce the rigidity of the aggregate supply curve for black agricultural economists. Since the agricultural economics profession is trending towards the

Ph.D. training level, it is important to identify the major obstacles encountered by blacks in obtaining such a degree. COSBAE's study found that blacks faced different problems in their pursuit of Ph.D. degrees than nonblacks. Blacks were almost five times as likely as their nonblack counterparts to cite financial problems as a major obstacle to completion of a Ph.D. degree. The source and level of financial assistance were also significantly different for black and nonblack Ph.D. candidates. While research and teaching assistantships were the primary source of financial support for nonblack Ph.D. students, black students on the other hand relied heavily on fellowships and salary from positions away from the parent department for support. This discrepancy in sources of financial support might be related to the high priority given to the Graduate Record Examination (GRE) scores in awarding teaching and research assistantships, and the tendency for blacks to be noncompetitive with whites on this test. Findings suggest, however, that serious reconsiderations should be given to the use of GRE scores as the primary criteria for granting graduate admission or financial assistance to blacks. Some graduate agricultural economics departments reported innovative programs for granting admission and financial support to black students based on criteria other than the GRE scores. In such cases, these departments reported no significant difference in the attrition rates of black and white graduate students, irrespective of GRE test scores. This finding suggests that the GRE score might not be a good predictor of success rate for black graduate students.

The agricultural economics profession must find innovative and pragmatic ways of providing increased financial assistance to black graduate students if it is genuinely concerned about the supply of black professionals. The scarcity of adequate financial support for black Ph.D. candidates is probably interacting with other factors to make the opportunity costs of possessing a Ph.D. degree extremely high for black agricultural economists. Opportunity costs were ranked second by blacks as a major obstacle to completing the Ph.D. degree. In recent years, the rate of return to accumulated human capital for blacks has risen sharply at all educational levels, but still remains low relative to whites. Since black Ph.D. agricultural economists are "crowded" into predominantly black academic institutions, with lower average salaries than nonblack institutions, this institutional factor could mitigate against increasing rates of return for accumulated black human capital stocks.

Thus, in addition to providing increased and competitive financial support to black Ph.D. candidates, the agricultural economics profession should seek ways of "widening" the market for these professionals. Such efforts would include "good faith" and aggressive efforts to eliminate artificial entry barriers to blacks qualified to fill faculty positions at predominantly white institutions. In undertaking these efforts, the profession should focus on the long-term benefits of a fuller participation of blacks in the profession. In short, it should not retreat from the philosophy of Equal Employment Opportunity and Affirmative Action because of the shorter-term political expediencies.

It is recognized that tight agricultural economics budget could pose a major constraint to increased and competitive financial support for black graduate students. However, joint-venture support programs between public and private organizations could be explored as a means of financing graduate programs for blacks. Such a program could be developed within the context of a National Needs Fellowship Program similar to the recently funded U.S. Department of Agriculture (USDA) program in the area of marketing. Such a fellowship program would, in the long run, assist in reducing the high opportunity costs of accumulated human capital stocks for black agricultural economists.

Demand Dimensions

The aggregate demand function for black agricultural economists would be conditioned in part by the derived demand for specific types of accumulated human capital stocks by firms and agencies employing agricultural economists. It is important, therefore, to determine if there are major divergences between the training of black agricultural economists and nonblack agricultural economists with respect to the skills demanded by potential employers. The study by Blank (1985) suggests that at the undergraduate level, the agribusiness option is projected to remain the high growth area over the decade. The trend would suggest that *ceteris paribus*, blacks with undergraduate degrees in this area should find lucrative employment opportunities in firms and agencies seeking this type of expertise. There are strong indications that this has indeed occurred. Black agribusiness majors with B.S. degrees are recruited heavily from 1890 institutions by agribusiness firms. Furthermore, the average entry level salaries offered to these degree holders are in most cases significantly higher than the current salaries of many M.S. and Ph.D. level agricultural economists. Undoubtedly, this trend will continue to adversely affect the pool of black undergraduate agricultural economics majors electing to pursue graduate degrees. At these relatively high B.S. salary levels, the opportunity costs are simply too high for them to pursue graduate level degrees. In addition, given the projected high growth demand in the South for undergraduate degree holders in marketing and farm management/production areas, these two areas could offer excellent additional employment opportunities for blacks holding B.S. degrees in these areas who would prefer to reside in the South. Given these trends, it would appear that the current subject matter orientation of black undergraduate agricultural economics students are in line with the high demand undergraduate areas. This is an economic factor that will mitigate against efforts to recruit these students into graduate agricultural economics programs.

At the graduate level there is a high projected demand for the traditional agricultural economics areas. It was suggested that the differences in the demand characteristics of graduate and undergraduate areas reflect differences in the projected demand for types of human capital stocks (Blank, 1985). An important policy question is whether black agricultural economists at the M.S. and Ph.D. levels are specializing in those subject matter areas that exhibit high demand potential. COSBAE's study found that black agricultural economists at the M.S. and Ph.D. levels are specializing in those subject matter areas with high growth demand potential. Specifically, black Ph.D. agricultural economists were more likely to specialize in farm management/production economics, marketing, and community resources. The study also found that blacks at the M.S. level were more likely to specialize in marketing and international trade/development.

The sectoral distribution of employment for black agricultural economists can be characterized as follows: (1) very few blacks employed as agricultural economists in private firms and agencies, (2) black agricultural economists employed by private firms and agencies tend to be hired at the B.S. and M.S. levels, (3) black Ph.D. agricultural economists are most likely to find academic employment at predominantly black institutions, and (4) next to predominantly black 1890 universities, the USDA is the only other public agency employing appreciable numbers of black Ph.D. and M.S. level agricultural economists.

It should be expected that the historically small pool of black agricultural economists would, to some degree, account for their underrepresentation in the various employment sectors. The most frequently given reason by employing agencies for not hiring black agricultural economists was their inability to find "qualified blacks." However, the small pool of blacks notwithstanding, it appears plausible to assume that since black agricultural economists possess the necessary skills for high demand areas, their sectoral employment distribution would be less concentrated than the data indicate. In particular, an important policy question is why have black Ph.D. agricultural economists failed to secure employment at academic institutions other than predominantly black institutions?   There are some indications that predominantly white academic institutions tend to view black Ph.D. agricultural economists as a differentiated product. As such, they might be applying different employment criteria for black and white applicants, which might mitigate against the hiring of black applicants. COSBAE's study found that predominantly white institutions assigned the highest priority to "levels of academic training" when making hiring decisions on Ph.D. agricultural economists, *regardless* of whether the position was for teaching, research, or extension positions. However, many predominantly white universities which received applications from black Ph.D. agricultural economists for teaching, research and extension positions, rejected such applicants on the basis of "poor research skills." This appears inconsistent, however, with their stated ranking of employment criteria, since research skill and teaching experience were ranked below academic training and supportive references for teaching and extension positions. Data strongly suggest that black Ph.D. agricultural economists have acquired high levels of subject matter training comparable to their white counterparts. Thus, to the extent that they are viewed as a differentiated product, and are subjected to different hiring criteria by predominantly white academic institutions, their employment opportunities are limited at such institutions.

Conclusions

A number of environmental program changes are occurring in the agricultural economics profession, and these changes are impacting the supply and demand characteristics of agricultural economists. Black agricultural economists, as a subset of agricultural economists, are impacted to varying degrees by these environmental changes. Historically, the supply curve for black agricultural economists has been fairly rigid in the outward direction. Furthermore, the supply curve shows limited potential for becoming less outwardly rigid in the near future.

A number of related factors are responsible for the inability of the agricultural economics profession to register positive growth in the supply of black agricultural economists. These factors are, among other things: (1) inability to attract a significant number of blacks into undergraduate agricultural economics programs, (2) limited financial support for black graduate students, (3) emphasis on the GRE scores as a primary criteria for admission to graduate programs, (4) high opportunity costs of graduate training for blacks, and (5) limitation of employment opportunities for black professionals with high accumulated human capital stocks.

On the demand side, the agricultural economics labor force appears to be segmented, particularly in the academic sector. Market segmentation appears to be maintained by employers' perception of blacks, particularly those with Ph.D. training, as a differentiated product from their white counterparts. As such, different and inconsistent hiring standards might be used to preclude blacks from gaining employment at institutions, other than those that are predominantly black with sizeable black clientele.

The agricultural economics profession must first exhibit courage in publicly recognizing the institutional impediments to increasing the supply of black agricultural economists. Second, the profession should invest some of its intellectual resources in seeking innovative and pragmatic ways of removing supply and demand constraints to the employment of black professionals. These are necessary steps to the improvement in the status and opportunities for black agricultural economists in the years ahead.

This paper reports policy implications of the study on opportunities and status of black agricultural economists, AAEA Occasional paper No. 4, June 1986.

References

Allen, J.E., C.G. Davis, S.H. Evans, W.E. Huffman, D. Jones, M. Nelson, A.L. Parks, and R.D. Robbins. *Opportunities and Status of Blacks in the Agricultural Economics Profession.* American Agricultural Economics Association, Occasional Paper No. 4. Ames, Iowa: American Agricultural Economics Association, June 1986, p. 53.

Beck, R., A. F. Bordeaux, J. T. Davis, R. H. Brannon, and L. L. Mather. 1977. "Undergraduate Programs in Agricultural Economics: Some Observations." *American Journal of Agricultural Economics* 59 (1977), pp. 766–768.

Blank, S. C. 1985. "A Decade of Change in Agricultural Economics Programs, 1975–1984." Paper presented at the annual meeting of the Northeastern Agricultural and Resource Economics Association, Amherst, Massachusetts, June 24–26, 1985.

Harl, N. E. 1983. "Agricultural Economics: Challenges to the Profession." *American Journal of Agricultural Economics* 65 (1983), pp. 845–854.

Polopolus, L. 1982. "Agricultural Economics Beyond the Farm Gate." *American Journal of Agricultural Economics* 64 (1982), pp. 803–810.

Contributors

JAMES T. BONNEN is professor of agricultural economics at Michigan State University. He received his B.A. in Economics from Texas A & M University, his M.A. in economics from Duke University, and a Ph.D. in Economics from Harvard University. Public policy, primarily for rural development and for agriculture, is the focus of his research and teaching. Bonnen served as chairman of the National Academy of Sciences Panel on Statistics for Rural Development Policy from 1979-80, director of the President's Federal Statistical System Reorganization Project from 1978 through 1980; as a member of the President's National Advisory Commission on Rural Poverty from 1966 through 1967; and as senior staff economist with the President's Council of Economic Advisers from 1963 through 1965. Elected president of the American Agricultural Economics Association in 1975, he was made fellow of that association in 1978. In 1984 he was elected fellow of the American Statistical Association.

MASON C. CARTER is dean of the College of Agriculture at Louisiana State University, and professor of forestry. In addition to normal academic interests his private consulting is in the areas of forestry and forest products; he serves on numerous academic and agribusiness committees and boards. Carter earned his B.S. in forestry at Virginia Polytechnic Institute, his M.S. in plant physiology, and his Ph.D. in forestry from Duke University. During his thirteen years at Auburn University, he progressed from assistant professor to Alumni Distinguished Professor. He then served as professor and head of the Department of Forestry and Natural Resources at Purdue for twelve years before spending two years as director of the Wood Utilization Research Center.

RALPH D. CHRISTY is associate professor of agricultural economics at Louisiana State University. His research and teaching interests are in agricultural marketing, economic development, and public policy. Christy earned his B.S. in agricultural economics (with honors) from Southern University and his M.S. and Ph.D. degrees in agricultural economics from Michigan State University. In 1989, he was visiting associate professor at Cornell University.

CARLTON G. DAVIS is professor in the Food and Resource Economics Department at the University of Florida. His teaching/research appointment is in human resource economics, food policy analyses, and international agricultural development. Davis earned his B.S. and M.S. degrees in agricultural economics from the University of Nebraska, and his Ph.D. degree in agricultural economics from Michigan State University. Davis was visiting Ford Foundation Scholar in the Department of Agricultural Economics and Farm Management at the University of the West Indies. He has extensive international experience and serves on numerous national committees.

SIDNEY H. EVANS is retired as associate dean for research in the School of Agriculture at North Carolina A & T State University. Before assuming this position, he was research director for the 1890 Evans-Allen Research Program, chairman of the Department of Agricultural Economics and Rural Sociology, and chairman of the Department of Economics. Evans received his B.S. degree in agricultural economics from Virginia State College, his M.S. degree in agricultural and general economics from Iowa State College, and his Ph.D. degree in agricultural economics from Ohio State University. In 1986, Evans received the George Washington Carver Public Service Award.

ALTON FRANKLIN has served as extension editor at North Carolina A&T State University since 1986. Prior to that (1981–1986), he worked as an editor at Wesley Medical Center in Wichita, Kansas. He received his B.A. in English from Tusculum College in Greeneville, Tennessee, and an M.F.A. in creative writing from Wichita State University.

FRED HUMPHERIES is president of Florida A & M University. He earned his B.S. (Magna Cum Laude) in chemistry from Florida A & M University in 1954. His Ph.D. is in Physical Chemistry from the University of Pittsburg, Pennsylvania, in 1964. Having begun his professional career as a commissioned officer in the U.S. Army, he served as president of Tennessee State University from 1974 to 1985, and has made significant contributions to higher education, in general, and to the higher education of blacks, specifically, through his service on many boards, committees, and commissions.   He has received numerous awards and honors for his leadership in the Land-Grant System.

WILLIAM P. HYTCHE is president of the University of Maryland—Eastern Shore, formerly known as Maryland State College. During his career at the University of Maryland—Eastern Shore, he has served as professor, chairman of the mathematics department, chairman of the Division of Liberal Studies, dean of student affairs, acting chancellor (1975), and chancellor (1976 to present). Hytche is the recipient of numerous honors and awards, including Academy of Arts and Science Fellow at Oklahoma State University, and the National Association for Equal Opportunities in Higher Education Distinguished Alumni of the Year Honors. He has also served as chairman of the Council of 1890 Land-Grant College Presidents.

MCKINLEY MAYES is coordinator of 1890 Colleges and Universities Programs for the Cooperative State Research Service, United States Department of Agriculture (USDA), Washington, D.C., where he is primarily responsible for the development and implementation of programs, policies, and procedures for the administration and coordination of federal research at the 1890 Land-Grant Institutions. Mayes received his B.S. degree from North Carolina A & T State University and his Ph.D. in agronomy from Rutgers University. After a long tenure as professor and associate dean, College of Agriculture, at Southern University, Baton Rouge, Louisiana, he accepted a position with the USDA (1976). He has served on many committees on research, extension, and resident instruction at the federal and state levels. Currently, he serves on the USDA/1890 Task Force, which was appointed by the secretary of agriculture to foster communication and cooperation between USDA agencies and the 1890 Land-Grant Universities.

DONALD MCDOWELL is associate professor in the Department of Agricultural Economics and Rural Sociology at North Carolina A & T State University. His responsibilities entail research and teaching in agricultural marketing, price analysis, and agribusiness management. An honors graduate of Southern University, McDowell received his M.S. and Ph.D. degrees from the University of Illinois in agricultural economics. He has completed short-term assignments in both Asia and Africa and has been visiting professor with Farmers Home Administration, Lincoln University, and the USDA/Economic Research Service. In 1986 he was a Kellogg Fellow with the National Center for Food and Agricultural Policy at Resources for the Future.

RIDGELEY A. MU'MIN is assistant professor in the Department of Agricultural Economics and Rural Sociology at North Carolina A&T State University. He received his Ph.D. from Michigan State University.

BENJAMIN F. PAYTON is president of Tuskegee University at Tuskegee, Alabama. He received his B.A. degree (with honors) from South Carolina State College, his B.D. degree from Harvard University, his M.A. degree from Columbia University, and his Ph.D. from Yale University. From 1963 through 1965 he served as director of the Community Research/Research Project and assistant professor at Howard University in Washington D.C. From 1965 through 1966 he served as director of the Department of Social Justice and the National Council of Churches in the USA. He was president of Benedict College in Columbia, South Carolina, from 1967 through 1972. From 1972 through 1981 he was program officer in education and public policy at the Ford Foundation. Currently, he serves as educational adviser to President George Bush, and team leader of the Presidential Task Force on Agricultural Development in Zaire. In addition, he is on numerous corporate boards and holds membership in a number of academic, civic and social organizations.

HUEL DAVIS PERKINS is executive to the chancellor at Louisiana State University. A graduate of Southern University, he holds the M.S. and Ph.D. degrees from Northwestern University in Evanston, Illinois. He serves on a number of local, state, and national committees—most recently as chairman of the Louisiana Endowment for the Humanities. He has over fifty articles and book reviews in print, and one speech he presented has been entered into the Congressional Record. He has worked at Lincoln University in Jefferson City, Missouri, at Southern University in Baton Rouge where he served as dean of the College of Arts and Humanities, and at Louisiana State University as vice-chancellor for academic affairs prior to receiving his current appointment.

MELVIN E. WALKER, JR. is acting president of Fort Valley State College. Prior to assuming that position, he served as dean and research director of the School of Agriculture, Home Economics, and Allied Programs, associate professor and research director of the Agricultural Research Station, and assistant professor of Agricultural Economics.

Walker received the A.S. degree from Prentiss Junior College, the B.S. degree in agriculture from Alcorn State University, and M.S. and Ph.D. degrees in agricultural economics from the University of Illinois. He has served as chairman of the Association of 1890 Research Directors and has received numerous honors and awards for his research in agricultural economics and rural sociology.

COLLIN C. WEIR is agricultural evaluation specialist with the International Science and Technology Institute in Washington, D.C. In this capacity, he supplies technical advisory support to the Research and University Relations Office, the Bureau of Science and Technology, and the Agency for International Development. Prior to that, he was director of International Agriculture Programs at Lincoln University in Missouri. Weir received his B.S. degree in agriculture, M.S. degree in soil chemistry from the University of Guelph, and Ph.D. in soil chemistry from the University of Manitoba, Canada.

CLIFTON R. WHARTON, JR. is chairman and chief executive officer of Teachers Insurance and Annuity Association and College Retirement Equities Funds, the nation's largest pension fund. Wharton has had an extensive career in foreign economic development, higher education, and business and is a recognized authority on economic development in Southeast Asia and Latin America. A graduate of Boston Latin School, he holds a B.A. degree in history from Harvard University. He has his M.A. degree in international affairs from Johns Hopkins University, School of Advanced International Studies, and his M.S. and Ph.D. degrees in economics from the University of Chicago. In addition, he holds thirty-five honorary degrees. He is a founding member of the Overseas Development Council and the first chairman of the board for International Food and Agricultural Development at the Agency of International Development (U.S. Department of State). He has served as chancellor of the State University of New York System, president of Michigan State University, and chairman of the Rockefeller Foundation.

HANDY WILLIAMSON, JR. is professor and head of the Department of Agricultural Economics and Rural Sociology at the University of Tennessee. From 1985 through early 1988, he was deputy director for research and university relations at the Bureau for Science and Technology, Agency for International Development, in Washington, D.C. He has held the positions of associate professor of agricultural economics, director of the Cooperative Agricultural Research Program, coordinator of international development activities at Tennessee State University, and associate director of the Center for Rural Development Research at Tuskegee University . Williamson received an A.A. degree in liberal arts from Pineywood Junior College, his B.S. degree in vocational agriculture from Alcorn State University, his M.S. degree in agricultural education from Tennessee State University and M.S. and Ph.D. degrees in agricultural economics from the University of Missouri.

LIONEL WILLIAMSON is associate professor of agricultural economics at the University of Kentucky, where he holds a joint appointment in teaching and extension. His assignments involve development, implementation, and evaluation of programs with a focus on agricultural cooperatives. Williamson has extensive international experience in East Africa and Indonesia. He earned his B.S. degree in agricultural education from Alcorn State University and his M.S. and Ph.D. degrees in agricultural economics from the University of Missouri at Columbia.

Abbreviations

AAEA	American Agricultural Economics Association
AID	Agency for International Development
ANE	Asia-Near East
BIFAD	Board for International Food and Agricultural Development
COSBAE	Committee on the Opportunities and Status of Blacks in Agricultural Economics
CRSP	Collaborative Research Support Program
CSRS	Cooperative State Research Service
ECOP	Extension Committee on Organization and Policy
ERS	Economic Research Service (USDA)
ESCOP	Experiment Station Committee on Organization and Policy
EO	Executive Order
FTE	Full Time Equivalents
GAO	U.S. General Accounting Office
HBCU	Historically Black Colleges and Universities
JMOU	Joint Memorandum of Understanding
LAC	Latin America and Caribbean
LDC	Less Developed Country
NAFEO	National Association for Equal Opportunity in Higher Education
NASULGC	National Association of State Universities and Land-Grant Colleges
PSG	Program Support Grant
PVO	Private Voluntary Organizations

RICOP   Resident Instruction Committee on Organization
                   and Policy
SGP   Strengthening Grant Program
USDA   U.S. Department of Agriculture

Index

163